The Sportsman's Catch

by
Leslie Delaney
St. Simons Publishing Co.

The Sportsman's Catch

3rd Printing

Leslie Delaney
St. Simons Publishing Co.
912-638-0309

ISBN 0-9671690-2-X

Introduction

The Sportsman's Catch is filled with more than 100 great recipes that will send you fishing or to the nearest fish market.

Cooks from coast to coast are always looking for new and creative ways to prepare fish and this cookbook is the answer.

This cookbook is informative on the various species of inshore and offshore fish.

Acknowledgements

Cover Art:
Alan James Robinson of Red Raven Graphics, Inc.

912-634-6315
Sport Fishing Apparel

Local Artist:
Jennifer Smith

Thanks to these fine sportsman's lodges for sharing their wonderful recipes:

The Lodge at Cabin Bluff, Sea Island, GA – 800-732-4752
Enon Plantation, Midway, AL – 334-529-3325
Henderson Village, Perry, GA – 888-615-9722
Wynfield Plantation, Albany, GA – 912-889-0193

Thanks to the Chefs and the Restaurants on Saint Simons Island for their recipes:

Delaney's Bistro–Chef Tom Delaney
Chelsea's–Kevin Pettingill
Chef David R. Snyder

Contents

Starters

~ Soups ~ Appetizers ~ Chowders ~ Soups ~ Appetizers ~ Chowders ~ Soups ~ Appeti
Chowders ~ Soups ~ Appetizers ~ Chowders ~ Soups ~ Appetizers ~ Chowders ~ Soups
etizers ~ Chowders ~ Soups ~ Appetizers ~ Chowders ~ Soups ~ Appetizers ~ Chowders ~ So
Appetizers ~ Chowders ~ Soups ~ Appetizers ~ Chowders ~ Soups ~ Appetizers ~ Chowders
ps ~ Appetizers ~ Chowders ~ Soups ~ Appetizers ~ Chowders ~ Soups ~ Appetizers ~ Chowe
So ps ~ Appetizers ~ Chowders ~ Soups ~ Appetizers ~ Chowders ~ Soups ~ Appetizers
wders ~ Soups ~ Appetizers ~ Chowders ~ Soups ~ Appetizers ~ Chowders ~ Soups ~ Appeti

Hot Crab Dip

1 (8-ounce) package cream cheese, softened	½ pound crabmeat
¼ cup milk	3 tablespoons chopped onion
⅓ cup mayonnaise	½ teaspoon garlic salt
1 teaspoon horseradish	Hot sauce to taste

Preheat oven to 350°. Combine all ingredients in a bowl. Spoon mixture into a casserole dish. Bake for 15 to 20 minutes. Serve with crackers.

Yield: 6 to 8 servings

Broiled Parmesan Cheese Oysters

1 pint oyster selects	1 tablespoon Old Bay seasoning
4 tablespoons butter, melted	¼ cup Parmesan cheese
Chopped garlic to taste	Salt and pepper to taste

Lay oysters on a broiler pan. Combine butter and garlic. Brush oysters with garlic butter and sprinkle with Old Bay seasoning, cheese, salt and pepper. Broil 5 to 6 minutes or until done.

Yield: 2 to 4 servings

Island Beer Brewed Oysters

1	(12-ounce) can beer	2	tablespoons Worcestershire sauce
2	pints oysters		Salt to taste
1	stick butter, melted		

Pour beer into a skillet. Add oysters, butter, Worcestershire sauce and salt. Cook over low heat until edges of oysters curl. Serve warm with crackers.

Yield: 6 to 8 servings

Oyster Fritters

2	cups all-purpose flour	1	cup milk
1	tablespoon baking powder	1	tablespoon oil
2	teaspoons salt	1	pint fresh oysters, drained and
1½	tablespoons Old Bay seasoning		chopped
2	eggs, beaten		Oil for frying

Sift together flour, baking powder, salt and Old Bay seasoning. In a mixing bowl, combine eggs, milk and 1 tablespoon oil. Add dry ingredients and stir until smooth. Mix in oysters. Drop batter by spoonfuls into hot oil. Fry about 3 to 5 minutes or until golden brown. Drain on paper towels.

Yield: 6 servings

Escargots Roquefort

32 extra large snails
1½ cups heavy cream
½ cup white wine

1 cup Roquefort cheese
Salt and pepper to taste

Combine heavy cream and wine in saucepan. Bring to a boil and reduce until thickened. Add Roquefort cheese, salt and pepper to taste. Serve with or in toasted French bread.

Yield: *4 servings*

Tomato-Crab Bisque

1 (28-ounce) can diced tomatoes
1 small Spanish onion, finely diced
4 tablespoons butter
½ cup flour
1½ quarts half-and-half

2 cups chicken broth
¼ cup dry sherry
Salt and white pepper to taste
8 ounces blue crab claw meat

Combine tomato and onion in a small saucepan and simmer 5 minutes. Whisk butter and flour in a medium saucepan over medium heat. Slowly add half-and-half. Whisk until sauce is smooth and simmering. Add chicken broth. Stir in tomato mixture. Cook 10 minutes, stirring frequently to avoid scorching. Bisque can be pureed at this point if a smoother texture is desired. Add sherry and season with salt and pepper. Fold crabmeat into soup and serve.

Yield: *6 to 8 servings*

I like it with chunks of tomatoes and Tom likes his pureed.

Oyster Stew

1	small onion, diced	1	quart half-and-half
4	tablespoons butter		Salt and pepper to taste
1	pint shucked oysters		

Sauté onion in butter in a saucepan until tender. Add oysters with some of the liquid, half-and-half, salt and pepper. Cook over low heat until hot. Do not bring to a boil.

Yield: 2 to 4 servings

Appalachacola Oyster Chowder

1	small onion, chopped	1	cup half-and-half
½	cup chopped celery	2	cups diced potatoes, cooked
4	tablespoons butter	1	cup corn
3	tablespoons flour		Salt and pepper to taste
2	cups milk	1	pint fresh oysters with liquid

Sauté onion and celery in butter until tender. Dust flour over sautéed vegetables. Stir in milk, half-and-half, potato, corn, salt and pepper. Heat mixture, stirring occasionally. Add oysters with liquid and heat 5 to 8 minutes or until oysters begin to curl. Do not boil.

Yield: 4 to 6 servings

Oyster-Mushroom Stew

1	pint small oysters	1	stick butter
	Milk	1	tablespoon dry sherry
1	(10¾-ounce) condensed cream of mushroom soup		Salt and pepper to taste

Drain oysters, reserving liquid. Add enough milk to liquid to equal 2 cups. In a medium saucepan, combine milk liquid, soup, butter, sherry, salt and pepper. Heat mixture, stirring occasionally. Add oysters and simmer 6 to 8 minutes or until oysters begin to curl.

Yield: 4 to 6 servings

Seafood Bounty Stew

1	slice bacon, diced	1	quart scallops (bay scallops preferred)
2	onions, diced	1	(8-ounce) can chopped clams, undrained
6	potatoes, peeled and cubed		
3	carrots, cubed	1	pound crabmeat
1½	pounds shrimp, peeled and deveined		Salt and pepper to taste
			Hot sauce to taste

Cook bacon in a large saucepan until crisp. Add onion and sauté until transparent. Add potatoes and carrots. Cover with water and cook 25 minutes or until vegetables are tender. Add shrimp and scallops and cook about 5 minutes. Add clams and crabmeat. Simmer about 20 minutes. Season to taste with salt, pepper and hot sauce. Goes great with cornbread.

Yield: 6 to 8 servings

Seafood Gumbo

1	onion, chopped	½	pound shrimp, peeled and deveined
1	red bell pepper, chopped		
1	green bell pepper, chopped	½	pound fresh fish
1	stalk celery, chopped	1	(6½-ounce) can chopped clams
1	tablespoon chopped garlic	1	cup chopped tasso or sausage
1	stick butter	½	(6½-ounce) bag frozen okra
½	cup flour	1	teaspoon thyme
8	cups broth	1	teaspoon Old Bay seasoning
1	(28-ounce) can diced tomatoes		Salt and pepper to taste

In a large pot, sauté onion, bell peppers, celery and garlic in butter until tender. Add flour and cook and stir to form a brown roux. Add broth and tomatoes. Simmer 20 minutes. Add shrimp, fish, clams, tasso, okra, thyme and Old Bay seasoning. Cook, stirring occasionally, until seafood is cooked. Season with salt and pepper. Serve over rice.

Yield: 6 to 8 servings

Shrimp Mull

8	slices bacon, diced	2	pounds shrimp, peeled and deveined
1	onion, diced		
6	baking potatoes, diced		Salt and pepper to taste
6	cups broth		

Sauté bacon until brown. Add onion and sauté until tender. Add potato and broth and cook until potatoes are al dente. Stir in shrimp and simmer until done. Season to taste with salt and pepper. Tastes best served with cornbread.

Yield: 4 servings

Cajun Clam Chowder

1	pound andouille sausage, diced	1	(28-ounce) can diced tomatoes
2	large onions, diced	4	large potatoes, diced
1	green bell pepper, diced	1	(10-ounce) can chopped clams,
1	cup all-purpose flour		undrained
1	quart half-and-half		Salt and pepper to taste
1	quart heavy cream		

In a large saucepan, cook sausage to render fat from sausage. Add onion and bell pepper and sauté about 5 minutes. Mix in flour and cook and stir for 2 minutes. Add half-and-half and cream. Mix well. Add tomatoes, potatoes and clams. Season to taste with salt and pepper. Cook until potatoes are tender.

Yield: 6 to 8 servings

Hatteras Clam Chowder

1	(10-ounce) can clams or 40 cherrystone (medium-size) clams	1	teaspoon black pepper
		1	teaspoon salt
2	cups diced potato	¼	teaspoon thyme
1	cup chopped celery	1	bay leaf
1	cup chopped onion	½	pound salt pork, cubed

Drain clams, reserving liquid. Chop clams and set aside. In a large stockpot, combine reserved clam liquid, potato, celery, onion, black pepper, salt, thyme, bay leaf and salt pork. Add enough water to cover vegetables by 3 to 4 inches. Cover stockpot and simmer until potatoes are tender. Remove bay leaf and salt pork. Stir in chopped clams.

Yield: 6 servings

Scallops Wrapped in Bacon

2   pints fresh scallops

12 slices bacon, cut in half

1   tablespoon Old Bay seasoning

    Salt and pepper to taste

Preheat oven to 450°. Place one scallop on half a slice of bacon. Sprinkle with Old Bay seasoning, salt and pepper. Roll bacon around scallop and secure with a wooden toothpick. Place on a baking pan. Repeat with remaining scallops. Bake about 10 minutes or until bacon is crisp.

Yield: 24 hors d'oeuvres

Shrimp Scampi

4   tablespoons butter

½ pound shrimp, peeled and deveined

2   tomatoes, diced

    Italian seasoning to taste

¼ cup minced garlic

8   ounces mushrooms, sliced

3   green onions, finely chopped

8   ounces dry linguine, cooked and drained

    Salt and pepper to taste

Melt butter in a large sauté pan. Add shrimp, tomatoes, Italian seasoning, garlic, mushrooms and onions. Sauté until shrimp are done. Add pasta and toss to mix. Season with salt and pepper.

Yield: 2 to 3 servings

Shrimp Ceviche

1½	pounds peeled shrimp	3	medium tomatoes, chopped
2	cups lemon juice	½	cup chopped cilantro
¼	cup dry vermouth	1	tablespoon hot pepper sauce
1	cup sliced red onion		Salt and pepper to taste

Combine shrimp, lemon juice, vermouth, onion, tomato, cilantro, pepper sauce, salt and pepper in a glass mixing bowl. Mix well and cover tightly. Refrigerate at least 24 hours.

Yield: 4 to 6 servings

Savannah Shrimp Spread

½	pound cooked shrimp, finely chopped	½	cup Parmesan cheese
1	(13-ounce) can artichoke hearts, drained and finely chopped	½	tablespoon minced garlic
		½	teaspoon cayenne pepper
¾	cup mayonnaise		Salt and pepper to taste

Preheat oven to 425°. Combine shrimp, artichoke, mayonnaise, cheese, garlic and cayenne pepper in a bowl. Season with salt and pepper. Transfer mixture to a shallow baking dish. Bake 10 minutes or until bubbly. Serve with crackers or chips.

Yield: 4 cups

Lobster and Crab Chowder

1	stick butter	1	tablespoon thyme
1	large onion, chopped	1	cup heavy cream
1	cup diced celery	½	pound crabmeat
⅔	cup flour	1	cup cooked and diced lobster
1½	quarts lobster stock	1	tablespoon Old Bay seasoning
2	medium potatoes, diced		Salt and pepper to taste
3	bay leaves		

Melt butter in a large saucepan over medium-high heat. Add onion and celery and sauté about 5 minutes. Mix in flour and cook about 5 minutes. Add stock, potatoes, bay leaves and thyme. Cook until potatoes are tender. Add cream and heat but do not boil. Stir in crabmeat, lobster, Old Bay seasoning, salt and pepper.

Yield: 4 to 6 servings

Clams Casino

24	clams in the shell	2	tablespoons chopped pimento
6	slices bacon, chopped	1	tablespoon Worcestershire sauce
1	small onion, chopped	¼	cup white wine
4	tablespoons butter		Salt and pepper to taste
1	tablespoon minced garlic		

Preheat oven to 450°. Clean and shuck clams, saving half of the shells. Place shells in boiling water for 5 minutes. Sauté bacon until crisp in a skillet. Add onion, butter, garlic, pimento, Worcestershire sauce, wine, salt and pepper. Cook about 5 minutes, stirring occasionally. Meanwhile, place clams on cleaned shells. Arrange shells in a baking pan. Spoon bacon mixture over clams. Bake 10 to 15 minutes.

Yield: 4 to 6 servings

Offshore Game Fish

Hatteras Grilled Dolphin with Tomato Salsa

Tomato Salsa

1	red onion, diced	1	tablespoon vinegar
1	tablespoon minced garlic	4	tomatoes, finely chopped
1	hot pepper, seeded and diced		Salt and pepper to taste
¼	cup chopped cilantro		

Dolphin

4	(6- to 8-ounce) dolphin steaks		Salt and pepper to taste
2	tablespoons vegetable oil		

Combine onion, garlic, hot pepper, cilantro and vinegar in a food processor. Process briefly. Transfer mixture to a mixing bowl. Stir in tomatoes and season with salt and pepper. To prepare dolphin, preheat grill. Rub dolphin steaks with oil and season with salt and pepper. Arrange steaks on grill rack. Grill for about 10 minutes, turning once or twice. Transfer to a serving platter. Spoon some salsa onto each steak and serve remaining salsa on the side.

Yield: 4 servings

Broiled Dolphin with Honey

4	(8-ounce) dolphin steaks	3	tablespoons honey
	Salt and pepper to taste	3	tablespoons olive oil
1	tablespoon Old Bay seasoning		

Preheat broiler. Season dolphin steaks with salt, pepper and Old Bay seasoning. Rub steaks on both sides with honey, then with oil. Place steaks on a nonstick baking sheet. Broil 4 to 5 minutes on each side.

Yield: 4 servings

Orange Ginger Glazed Grilled Dolphin

4	(6- to 8-ounce) dolphin steaks	1	tablespoon grated fresh ginger
½	cup oil	1	tablespoon soy sauce
½	cup orange marmalade		Salt and pepper to taste
½	cup Dijon mustard		

Combine all ingredients in a dish and mix well. Marinate 1 to 2 hours. When ready to cook, preheat grill. Remove steaks from marinade, reserving marinade. Place steaks on grill rack, not directly over flames to prevent burning. Grill for about 10 minutes, turning once or twice. Brush with remaining marinade while cooking.

Yield: 4 servings

Dog Island Grilled Dolphin with Cilantro Butter

Cilantro Butter

1	stick unsalted butter, softened	1	teaspoon lemon or lime zest
¼	cup chopped cilantro		Salt and pepper to taste
	Juice of 1 lemon or lime		

Dolphin

4	(8-ounce) dolphin steaks		Salt and pepper to taste
	Olive oil		

Combine all cilantro butter ingredients in a bowl. Mix by hand or with a mixer. Shape into a log. Wrap and freeze for about 1 hour. When ready to cook, preheat grill. Rub dolphin steaks with oil and season with salt and pepper. Grill steaks for about 10 minutes, turning once. Transfer to a serving platter and top each steak with a slice of cilantro butter.

Yield: 4 servings

Baked Dolphin with Dijon Dill Sauce

Dijon Dill Sauce

1 cup sour cream	¼ cup minced onion
½ cup yogurt	2 tablespoons Dijon mustard
½ cup chopped fresh dill weed	Salt and pepper to taste

Dolphin

4 (6-ounce) dolphin steaks   Salt and pepper to taste

Combine all sauce ingredients in a small bowl. Let stand at room temperature for 1 hour. When ready to cook, preheat oven to 425°. Arrange dolphin steaks in a greased baking pan. Season with salt and pepper. Spread some of sauce over steaks and bake 15 to 20 minutes. Serve steaks with remaining sauce on the side.

Yield: 4 servings

Dolphin with Lemon Saffron Sauce

4 (8-ounce) dolphin steaks	½ cup dry white wine
Juice of 1 lemon	1 cup clam juice
¼ cup olive oil, divided	½ teaspoon saffron threads
1 tablespoon minced garlic	1 stick butter
Salt and pepper to taste	

Place dolphin steaks in a baking dish. Pour lemon juice and 2 tablespoons olive oil over steaks. Sprinkle garlic on top. Turn steaks to coat. Let stand 30 minutes. Heat remaining 2 tablespoons oil in a sauté pan. Remove steaks from marinade and sauté in pan 4 to 5 minutes on each side. Meanwhile, combine wine, clam juice and saffron in a saucepan. Bring to a boil over medium heat and cook until reduced. Whisk in butter. Pour sauce over steaks.

Yield: 4 servings

Dolphin with Sun-Dried Tomato Sauce

Dolphin

4	(6- to 8-ounce) dolphin fillets	½	cup flour
1	tablespoon Old Bay seasoning	¾	cup vegetable oil
	Salt and pepper to taste		

Sun-Dried Tomato Sauce

1½	cups heavy cream	¼	cup chopped green onion
¼	cup diced sun-dried tomatoes	4	tablespoons butter
2	plum tomatoes, diced		

Sprinkle dolphin fillets evenly with Old Bay seasoning, salt and pepper. Dredge in flour. Sauté fillets in hot vegetable oil for 3 to 5 minutes on each side. Remove fillets and keep warm. To prepare sauce, bring cream to a boil in a saucepan and cook until reduced. Add tomatoes and green onion. Cook 3 minutes longer. Whisk in butter. Pour sauce over fillets.

Yield: 4 servings

Key West Dolphin Kebabs

½	cup olive oil	½	teaspoon black pepper
3	tablespoons chopped fresh dill weed	1½	pounds dolphin fillets, cubed
3	tablespoons brandy	1	red bell pepper, cubed
1	teaspoon salt	2	zucchini squash, cubed
		1	lemon, cut into wedges

In a large bowl, combine oil, dill, brandy, salt and pepper. Add dolphin and toss to mix. Cover and refrigerate for about 1 hour, mixing once or twice. When ready to cook, preheat grill. Remove fish from marinade, reserving marinade. To make kebabs, skewer dolphin, bell pepper and squash; repeat. Place kebabs on grill. Grill 8 to 10 minutes or until done, turning and brushing with marinade while cooking. Serve with lemon wedges.

Yield: 4 to 6 servings

Teriyaki Dolphin

½ cup soy sauce
¼ cup dry sherry
1 tablespoon sugar

2 tablespoons grated fresh ginger
1 clove garlic, crushed
4 (6- to 8-ounce) dolphin steaks

Combine soy sauce, sherry, sugar, ginger and garlic. Pour over dolphin steaks. Cover and refrigerate 30 minutes or up to 2 hours, turning occasionally. Preheat a grill or broiler. Remove steaks from marinade, reserving marinade. Grill or broil steaks 2 to 3 minutes on each side, basting with marinade while cooking.

Yield: 4 servings

Gulf Stream Yellowfin Blackened Tuna

2 tablespoons paprika
1 tablespoon cayenne pepper
3 tablespoons Old Bay seasoning

1 tablespoon ground cumin
3 tablespoons butter
4 (8-ounce) tuna steaks

Combine paprika, cayenne pepper, Old Bay seasoning and cumin in a flat dish. Heat a large skillet over high heat. Melt butter in skillet. Dip both sides of each tuna steak in spice mixture, patting spices in by hand. Place steaks in skillet and cook 3 to 4 minutes on each side, turning carefully.

Yield: 4 servings

Bluefin Oriental-Style Tuna

1½	cups soy sauce	1	teaspoon sugar
½	cup white wine	1	teaspoon grated fresh ginger
2	tablespoons water	4	(6- to 8-ounce) tuna steaks

Combine soy sauce, wine, water, sugar and ginger in a dish. Add tuna and marinate for 1 hour. When ready to cook, preheat broiler. Remove steaks from marinade and broil 4 inches from heat source for 12 to 15 minutes. Serve with stir-fried vegetables.

Yield: 4 servings

Bluefin Jalapeño Glazed Tuna Steaks

1	cup pepper jelly		Juice of 1 lime
½	cup chopped fresh cilantro		Salt and pepper to taste
3	tablespoons wine vinegar	4	(7- to 8-ounce) tuna steaks
1	jalapeño pepper, seeded and mined		

Combine jelly, cilantro, vinegar, jalapeño pepper, lime juice, salt and pepper in a saucepan. Bring to a simmer and cook about 10 minutes. Cool. Pour three-fourths of glaze mixture over tuna steaks and refrigerate for about 1 hour. When ready to cook, preheat grill. Remove steaks from marinade, reserving marinade to use as a baste. Place steaks on grill and baste with marinade. Grill 5 to 8 minutes or until done. Serve with remaining one-fourth of glaze.

Yield: 4 servings

Blackened Tuna with Pineapple Black Bean Salsa

2	cups cooked black beans	½	cup pineapple juice
2	cups diced pineapple	¼	cup vinegar
½	cup diced red bell pepper	½	cup chopped parsley
½	cup diced yellow bell pepper		Salt and pepper to taste
¼	cup diced red onion	4-6	(7- to 8-ounce) tuna steaks
2	tablespoons chopped scallions	1	cup blackening spice
¼	cup chopped fresh thyme or cilantro		Sprigs of fresh cilantro for garnish

To prepare salsa, combine black beans, pineapple, bell peppers, onion, scallions, thyme, pineapple juice, vinegar and parsley in a mixing bowl. Season with salt and pepper and refrigerate at least 2 hours. When ready to serve, heat a cast iron pan over low heat for about 10 minutes. Dust tuna steaks with blackening spice. Sear steaks to desired degree of doneness. Serve tuna with salsa and garnish with cilantro.

Yield: 4 to 6 servings

Oregon Inlet
Grilled Yellowfin Tuna

1   cup mayonnaise
½   cup teriyaki sauce
1   tablespoon minced fresh ginger

1   tablespoon minced garlic
4   (8-ounce) tuna steaks

Combine mayonnaise, teriyaki sauce, ginger and garlic in a dish. Mix well. Add tuna steaks and marinate 1½ hours in refrigerator. When ready to cook, preheat grill. Remove steaks from marinade, reserving marinade. Grill steaks 3 minutes on each side, basting with marinade while cooking.

Yield: 4 servings

Bluefin Tuna Sautéed
with Brown Butter

¾   cup flour
    Salt and pepper to taste
4   (7-ounce) tuna steaks
¼   cup vegetable oil

4   tablespoons butter
1   teaspoon chopped fresh tarragon
1   teaspoon chopped fresh thyme

Combine flour, salt and pepper in a flat dish. Dredge tuna steaks in seasoned flour. Sauté steaks in hot vegetable oil in a large sauté pan for 3 to 6 minutes on each side. Transfer to a serving platter and keep warm. Melt butter in a small sauté pan over medium heat. Swirl pan until butter lightly browns. Spoon butter over steaks and sprinkle with tarragon and thyme.

Yield: 4 servings

Henderson Village Hot and Sour Seared Yellowfin Tuna with a Bacon Asparagus and New Potato Salad and Green Pesto

2	tablespoons rice wine vinegar	½	pound hickory bacon, finely chopped
2	tablespoons sugar		
1	teaspoon soy sauce	1	pound asparagus, roughly chopped
1	chili pepper, finely diced		
1	tablespoon sesame oil	1	pound new potatoes, cooked and cubed
1	small piece fresh ginger, finely chopped	1	Vidalia onion, finely chopped
8	(6-ounce) pieces tuna	1	teaspoon horseradish sauce

Green Pesto

1	large bunch basil	4	cloves garlic
2	tablespoons pine nuts	2	ounces grated Parmesan cheese
10	tablespoons olive oil	2	tablespoons white wine

Combine vinegar, sugar, soy sauce, chili pepper, sesame oil and ginger in a small saucepan. Bring to a boil, reduce heat and simmer 5 minutes. Remove from heat and chill. Place tuna in a shallow dish, cover with chilled dressing and marinate 2 hours. Lightly oil a wok and heat until very hot. Fry bacon and onion for a few minutes. Add asparagus and cook for a few minutes. Turn off heat, add potatoes and horseradish and mix lightly. Season to taste. For Pesto: Combine all ingredients in a food processor and process until smooth. Grill tuna to your liking. To serve, place asparagus salad in a large bowl. Top with tuna and drizzle with pesto.

Carolina Garlic Skewered Yellowfin Tuna

8	large heads garlic	1	teaspoon Old Bay seasoning
2	tablespoons minced garlic	½	teaspoon salt
½	cup olive oil		Cayenne pepper to taste
⅓	cup tomato sauce	2	pounds tuna, cut into 1-inch
¼	cup wine vinegar		cubes

Blanch whole garlic heads in boiling water for 5 minutes. Drain and set aside. Combine minced garlic, olive oil, tomato sauce, vinegar, Old Bay seasoning, salt and cayenne pepper in a large bowl. Mix well. Add tuna and refrigerate about 1 hour, tossing twice. When ready to cook, preheat grill. Remove tuna from marinade, reserving marinade. Skewer tuna and individual garlic cloves. Place skewers on grill and cook 5 to 6 minutes, turning frequently and basting with marinade while cooking.

Yield: 4 to 6 servings

Yellowfin Tuna with Mustard Basil Butter

1	stick unsalted butter, softened	4	(8-ounce) tuna steaks
2	tablespoons Dijon mustard		Vegetable oil
3	tablespoons chopped fresh basil		Salt and pepper to taste

Preheat grill. Combine butter, mustard and basil in a small bowl. Rub tuna steaks with vegetable oil and season with salt and pepper. Grill steaks about 3 minutes on each side. Top each steak with butter before serving.

Yield: 4 servings

Seared Tuna over Coconut Basmati and Asian Slaw

Tuna and Rice

4	(6-ounce) center cut tuna steaks	2	cups basmati rice
1	teaspoon salad oil	1	(8-ounce) can coconut milk
1	teaspoon sesame oil	1	teaspoon ground ginger
1	teaspoon butter	2	cups water
¼	yellow onion, diced		Salt and pepper to taste

Asian Slaw

2	cups sliced napa or green cabbage	¼	bunch cilantro, sliced
1	red bell pepper, julienned		Sesame Soy Vinaigrette
1	carrot, julienned		(see recipe below)
1	bunch scallions, sliced		

Over high heat, sear tuna in salad and sesame oils for 30 seconds on each side. Transfer tuna to a plate and set aside at room temperature. Reduce heat to low and add butter to pan. Add onion and sweat 5 minutes without browning. Stir in rice and sweat 2 minutes longer, being careful to prevent browning. Increase to high heat and add coconut milk, ginger and water. Season with salt and pepper and bring to a boil. Reduce heat to low, cover, and cook about 15 minutes or until rice is tender. To prepare slaw, combine cabbage, bell pepper, carrot, scallions and cilantro. Toss with vinaigrette. When ready to serve, cut tuna into thin slices. Mound rice on serving plates, surrounded by slaw. Place tuna on rice and serve.

Yield: 4 servings

Sesame Soy Vinaigrette

½	cup soy sauce	1	tablespoon sesame seeds, toasted
¼	cup rice vinegar	1	cup salad oil
	Juice of 2 limes		Pinch of cayenne pepper
2	tablespoons sesame oil		

Combine all ingredients and blend.

Grilled Yellowfin Tuna with Red Onions

½	cup garlic-flavored olive oil		Salt and pepper to taste
	Juice of 1 lemon	2	pounds yellowfin tuna, cut into
2	tablespoons chopped fresh		1-inch cubes
	rosemary	24	1x1x¼-inch red onion pieces

Whisk together oil, lemon juice, rosemary, salt and pepper in a small bowl. Add tuna and marinate at least 30 minutes. Preheat grill to medium heat. Thread tuna and onion onto metal skewers. Season with salt and pepper. Grill 8 minutes or until tuna is just opaque in the center, basting often with marinade.

Yield: 4 servings

Tuna Steaks with Tomatoes

4	tablespoons olive oil, divided		Salt and pepper to taste
1	tablespoon sesame oil	1½	cups halved cherry tomatoes
4	(8-ounce) tuna steaks, 1 inch		Juice of ½ lime
	thick	1	tablespoon grated ginger

Combine 2 tablespoons olive oil with sesame oil. Brush oil mixture over steaks. Season well with salt and pepper. Toss tomato halves with remaining 2 tablespoons olive oil, lime juice, ginger, salt and pepper. Coat grill rack with cooking spray and preheat grill to medium-high heat. Grill steaks to desired degree of doneness. Transfer to individual plates and top with tomato mixture. Serve immediately.

Yield: 4 servings

Broiled Bluefin Tuna with Garlic and Mint

4	(6- to 8-ounce) tuna steaks	2	tablespoons chopped fresh mint
	Salt and pepper to taste	1	tablespoons chopped fresh parsley
2	tablespoons minced garlic		Lemon wedges

Season tuna steaks with salt and pepper. Rub both sides of steaks with garlic, mint and parsley. Marinate 1 hour. When ready to cook, preheat broiler. Place steaks on a greased nonstick baking pan. Broil steaks 4 to 5 minutes on each side. Serve with lemon wedges.

Yield: 4 servings

Grilled Bluefin Tuna Balsamico

½	cup balsamic vinegar	½	teaspoon salt (optional)
½	cup olive oil	¼	teaspoon black pepper
2	large cloves garlic or to taste, crushed	6	(¾-inch thick) tuna steaks

Whisk together vinegar, oil, garlic, salt and pepper to make a marinade. Place steaks in a glass baking dish. Pour marinade over steaks. Cover and refrigerate for 30 minutes or up to 4 hours, turning steaks occasionally. When ready to cook, preheat grill. Remove steaks from marinade and grill 2 minutes on each side.

Yield: 6 servings

Amelia Island King Fish Au Gratin

4   (6- to 8-ounce) king mackerel
   steaks
   Salt and pepper to taste
¼   cup olive oil

¾   cup bread crumbs
¾   cup grated Parmesan cheese
4   tablespoons butter

Preheat oven to 375°. Place steaks in a greased baking pan. Season with salt and pepper. Drizzle oil over steaks. Cover steaks with bread crumbs, then sprinkle with cheese. Place 1 tablespoon butter on top of each steak. Bake 20 to 25 minutes or until done.

Yield: 4 servings

Grilled Lemon Butter King Mackerel Fish Steaks

¾   cup melted butter
   Juice of 1 lemon
2   tablespoons chopped fresh parsley

   Salt and pepper to taste
4   (6- to 8-ounce) king mackerel
   steaks

Combine butter, lemon juice, parsley, salt and pepper. Place steaks in a dish. Pour mixture over steaks and chill 1 to 2 hours. When ready to cook, preheat grill. Brush steaks twice with mixture and then place on grill. Cook 7 to 10 minutes or until done.

Yield: 4 servings

Baked King Mackerel

4	(1½- to 2-inch thick) king mackerel steaks	2	tablespoons chopped fresh chives
1	cup sour cream		Juice of 1 lemon
½	cup mayonnaise		Salt and pepper to taste

Preheat oven to 400°. Place steaks in a greased baking dish. Combine sour cream, mayonnaise, chives and lemon juice in a small bowl. Spread mixture over steaks. Season with salt and pepper. Bake 20 to 30 minutes.

Yield: 4 servings

Stuart Grilled Wahoo with Anchovy Lemon Butter

4	tablespoons butter, softened		Juice of ½ a lemon
1	(2-ounce) can anchovy fillets, minced	1	teaspoon lemon zest
1	tablespoon minced shallots	4	(6- to 8-ounce) wahoo fillets
			Salt and pepper to taste

Preheat grill. Use a fork to mash together butter, anchovy fillets, shallots, lemon juice and zest. Season wahoo fillets with salt and pepper. Grill fillets 8 to 12 minutes. Transfer to a serving plate and top fillets with anchovy butter.

Yield: 4 servings

Wahoo with Herb Crust

1 cup herb stuffing mix	4 (6- to 8-ounce) wahoo fillets
¼ cup chopped fresh parsley	¼ cup melted butter
Zest of 1 lemon	Salt and pepper to taste

Preheat oven to 450°. Place stuffing mix, parsley and zest in a food processor and blend to a fine consistency. Pour mixture into a dish. Brush wahoo fillets with some of butter and season with salt and pepper. Dredge fillets in crumb mixture to coat. Place fillets in a baking dish and drizzle with remaining butter. Bake about 15 to 20 minutes.

Yield: 4 servings

Bluewater Wahoo with Leeks and Tomatoes

4 (6- to 8-ounce) wahoo fillets	1 tablespoon minced garlic
Salt and pepper to taste	4 plum tomatoes, chopped
3 tablespoons olive oil	1 teaspoon dried tarragon
2 medium leeks, white only, thinly sliced	1 teaspoon balsamic vinegar

Preheat oven to 375°. Season wahoo fillets with salt and pepper and place in a glass baking dish. Heat oil in a large sauté pan over medium heat. Add leeks and garlic and sauté for about 5 minutes. Add tomatoes and tarragon and cook about 3 minutes. Add vinegar and season with salt and pepper. Spoon mixture over fillets and bake about 18 to 20 minutes.

Yield: 4 servings

Red Snapper Au Poivre

1	teaspoon kosher salt	½	teaspoon dried thyme
1	teaspoon whole white peppercorns	6	(6- to 8-ounce) red snapper fillets with skin
1	teaspoon whole black peppercorns	3	tablespoons olive oil
½	teaspoon red pepper flakes	½	cup melted unsalted butter
		⅓	cup chopped Italian parsley

Grind salt, peppercorns, pepper flakes and thyme together in a spice mill. Coat snapper fillets with seasoning mixture. Heat a cast iron pan over high heat. When very hot, add 1 tablespoon of oil to pan and tilt to coat. Immediately place 2 fillets in pan and cook 1 to 2 minutes. Turn and cook for another minute. Transfer to a serving platter and keep warm while cooking remaining fillets. Brush cooked fillets with melted butter and sprinkle with parsley.

Yield: 6 servings

Red Snapper with Old Bay, Dill, Capers and Lemon

4	(6- to 8-ounce) red snapper fillets	2	tablespoons chopped fresh dill weed
¼	cup Old Bay seasoning	4	tablespoons butter
	Flour		Juice of 1 lemon
	Black pepper to taste	2	tablespoons capers or to taste

Preheat oven to 350°. Sprinkle one side of each snapper fillet with Old Bay seasoning. Dust with flour and pepper and sprinkle with dill. Melt butter in a non-stick skillet over medium heat. Add fillets and brown on both sides. Transfer fillets and butter to a glass baking dish. Add lemon juice and capers. Bake 5 to 10 minutes or until done. Serve immediately.

Yield: 4 servings

Seaside Sautéed Red Snapper Topped with Crabmeat

½	cup flour	1	cup heavy cream
	Salt and pepper to taste	¼	cup green onions
½	tablespoon Old Bay seasoning	½	cup crabmeat
4	(6- to 8-ounce) red snapper fillets	1½	tablespoons dry sherry
½	cup vegetable oil		

Combine flour, salt, pepper and Old Bay seasoning in a dish. Dredge snapper fillets in mixture. Heat oil in a sauté pan over medium-high heat. Add fillets and cook about 5 to 8 minutes on each side. Meanwhile, in a saucepan, bring cream to a boil and cook to reduce. Add onions, crabmeat and sherry. Season with salt and pepper to taste. Serve sauce over fillets.

Yield: 4 servings

Baked Red Snapper with Wine and Herbs

4	(6- to 8-ounce) red snapper fillets	1	bay leaf
	Salt and pepper to taste	1	cup dry white wine
1	cup chopped mushrooms		Juice of 1 lemon
¼	cup chopped shallots	½	cup clam juice
1	teaspoon chopped garlic	1½	sticks butter, divided
½	teaspoon dried thyme		

Preheat oven to 450°. Place snapper fillets in a greased baking dish. Season with salt and pepper. Add mushrooms, shallots, garlic, thyme, bay leaf, wine, lemon juice and clam juice. Cut half stick of butter into 4 pieces and place on top of fillets. Bake 10 to 20 minutes. Pour liquid from dish into a small saucepan. Bring to a boil. Swirl in remaining stick of butter until melted, but do not boil. Serve sauce over fillets.

Yield: 4 servings

Red Snapper with Herb Butter

¼ cup olive oil
¼ cup melted unsalted butter
    Juice of 1 lemon
1 teaspoon chopped fresh thyme, or
    ½ teaspoon dried

3 tablespoons chopped fresh basil,
    or 1 tablespoon dried
1-2 tablespoons chopped garlic
4 (6- to 8-ounce) red snapper fillets
    Salt and pepper to taste

Combine oil, butter, lemon juice, thyme, basil and garlic in a bowl. Season snapper fillets generously with salt and pepper. Place fillets in a glass baking dish. Pour mixture over fillets. Cover fish with plastic and let stand at room temperature for 1 hour. When ready to cook, heat a large non-stick skillet over high heat. Remove fillets from marinade, reserving marinade. Place fillets, skin-side up, in skillet and cook for 1 minute. Turn fillets, cover tightly, and reduce heat to low. Cook about 8 minutes or until done. Pour marinade over fish and cook 1 minute longer. Serve immediately with marinade sauce over fish.

Yield: 4 servings

Sea Island Cobia Kebabs

¼ cup olive oil
1 tablespoon minced garlic
2 tablespoons chopped cilantro
2 tablespoons lime juice
1 (20-ounce) can pineapple
    chunks, juice reserved
    Salt and pepper to taste

1 pound cobia, cut into 1½-inch
    cubes
8 cherry tomatoes
1 green bell pepper, cut into 1-inch
    squares
1 red onion, cut into 1-inch chunks

Combine oil, garlic, cilantro, lime juice and reserved pineapple juice in a large bowl. Season with salt and pepper. Add cobia and marinate 1 hour. Soak bamboo skewers in water for 15 minutes. Preheat grill. Prepare kebabs by alternating cobia, pineapple, tomatoes, bell pepper and onion onto skewers. Grill until done.

Yield: 4 servings

Seared Cobia Pepper Steaks

2	tablespoons cracked black pepper	½	cup chopped shallots
4	(1¼-inch thick) cobia steaks	1	cup chicken broth
	Salt	¼	cup brandy
2	tablespoons olive oil		Salt and pepper to taste
1	stick unsalted butter		

Press cracked pepper evenly into cobia steaks. Sprinkle lightly with salt. Heat oil in a sauté pan over medium-high heat. Add steaks and sear 3 to 4 minutes on each side or until done. Transfer to a serving platter and keep warm. Add butter and shallots to same sauté pan. Cook about 4 minutes. Add broth and brandy. Bring to a boil and cook until sauce reduces. Season with salt and pepper. Spoon sauce over steaks.

Yield: 4 servings

Chili Seared Cobia

2	tablespoons chili powder	4	(6- to 8-ounce) cobia steaks
	Salt and pepper to taste		Oil for cooking

Combine chili powder, salt and pepper. Rub mixture evenly over steaks. Heat oil in a skillet over medium-high heat. Add steaks and cook 4 to 6 minutes on each side. Serve with Pickled Slaw or side dish of choice.

Yield: 4 servings

Pan Seared Pompano Coated with Sesame Seeds

4	tablespoons olive oil, divided		Salt and pepper to taste
1	tablespoon minced garlic	4	(6- to 8-ounce) pompano fillets
6	plum tomatoes, seeded, skinned and chopped	¼	cup sesame seeds
2	tablespoons chopped fresh basil	1	lemon, cut into wedges

Heat 2 tablespoons oil in a sauté pan. Add garlic and sauté 2 minutes. Add tomato, basil, salt and pepper. Cook 5 minutes. Keep warm. Season pompano fillets with salt and pepper. Coat both sides of fillets lightly with sesame seeds. Heat remaining 2 tablespoons oil in a large sauté pan over medium-high heat. Add fillets and cook 3 to 4 minutes on each side or until brown. Spoon tomato sauce over each fillet and garnish with lemon wedges.

Yield: 4 servings

Marlin Kebabs

4	pounds marlin, cut into 1½-inch cubes		Green bell pepper, cut into cubes
	Onion, cut into chunks		Cherry tomatoes
	Mushrooms	1½	cups of your favorite Italian dressing

Prepare kebabs by alternating pieces of marlin, onion, mushrooms, bell pepper and cherry tomatoes onto skewers. Place kebabs in a glass dish. Pour dressing over kebabs and marinate 1 to 2 hours. When ready to cook, preheat grill. Grill kebabs about 10 minutes, turning frequently while cooking. Serve over rice.

Yield: 10 to 12 servings

Braised Pompano and Golden Onions

4 tablespoons butter	Salt and pepper to taste
1 onion, thinly sliced	1 cup heavy cream
1 tablespoon dried thyme	½ cup dry white wine
4 (5- to 6-ounce) pompano fillets	

Melt butter in a medium sauté pan over medium heat. Add onion and cook 12 minutes or until golden, stirring frequently. Add thyme and cook 1 minute longer. Season pompano fillets with salt and pepper. Place fillets on top of onion. Add cream and wine, swirling pan to blend liquids. Bring to a simmer. Reduce heat to low and cover pan. Cook about 7 minutes. Transfer fillets to a serving platter and keep warm. Return pan to heat and bring sauce to a boil. Cook until slightly thickened. Spoon sauce over fillets.

Yield: 4 servings

Marlin with Hazelnuts

¾ cup hazelnuts, toasted	4 (6-ounce) marlin fillets
¼ cup flour	Salt and pepper to taste
1 tablespoon chopped fresh rosemary	1 egg, beaten
	4 tablespoons butter

Finely grind hazelnuts, flour and rosemary in a food processor. Pour mixture into a bowl. Season marlin fillets with salt and pepper. Dip fillets in egg, then dredge in flour mixture to coat. Sauté fillets in butter for about 3 to 5 minutes on both sides.

Yield: 4 servings

Marlin with Artichokes and Mushrooms

1   (6-ounce) jar marinated
    artichokes, marinade reserved
4   (7- to 8-ounce) marlin fillets
    Salt and pepper to taste
1   pound fresh mushrooms, halved

3   tablespoons chopped fresh basil
2   tablespoons minced garlic
¼   cup clam juice
¼   cup dry white wine

Preheat oven to 450°. Drain artichoke marinade into a glass bowl. Add marlin fillets, turning to coat. Season fillets with salt and pepper and place in a baking dish. Scatter artichokes, mushrooms, basil and garlic around fillets. Pour clam juice and wine over fillets. Bake 20 to 25 minutes or until done.

Yield: 4 servings

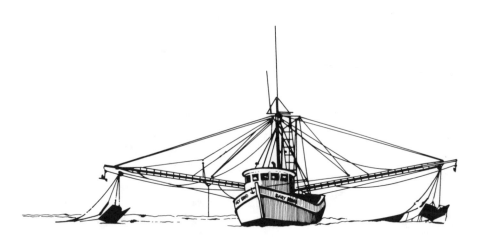

NOTES

Inshore Game Fish

St. Simon Speckled Trout with Tomatoes and Herbs

1	onion, julienned	2	teaspoons basil
1	green bell pepper, julienned	1	teaspoon oregano
1	tablespoon minced garlic	1	teaspoon red pepper flakes
¼	cup olive oil, divided		Juice of 1 lemon
2	(14½-ounce) cans chopped tomatoes	6	(6- to 8-ounce) trout fillets
			Salt and pepper to taste

Sauté onion, bell pepper and garlic in 2 tablespoons oil until tender. Add tomatoes, basil, oregano, pepper flakes and lemon juice. Simmer about 15 minutes. Meanwhile, sauté fillets, turning once, in remaining 2 tablespoons oil for 4 to 8 minutes or until done. Season with salt and pepper. Pour sauce over top.

Yield: 6 servings

Sautéed Speckled Trout

1	cup bread crumbs	¼	cup olive oil
1	cup Parmesan cheese	1	shallot, minced
1	pound trout fillets	1	tablespoon chopped garlic
2	eggs, beaten		

Combine crumbs and cheese in a bowl. Dip trout fillets in egg, then roll in crumb mixture. Heat oil in a sauté pan. Add shallot and sauté until tender. Add garlic and cook 2 minutes. Add fillets and cook, turning once, until golden brown.

Yield: 2 servings

Baked Grey Trout with Romano Cheese

1 cup bread crumbs	4 (8-ounce) trout fillets
1 tablespoon garlic powder	⅓ cup lemon juice
½ cup grated Romano cheese	¼ cup olive oil
½ cup chopped fresh parsley	

Preheat oven to 425°. Combine bread crumbs, garlic powder, cheese and parsley in a bowl. Rub fillets with lemon juice. Dredge fillets in crumb mixture to coat. Place fillets on a baking pan lined with wax or parchment paper. Drizzle oil over fillets. Bake in center of oven for 10 to 15 minutes or until done.

Yield: 4 servings

Grilled Speckled Trout with Herbs

8 sprigs fresh rosemary	¾ cup olive oil
8 sprigs fresh oregano	Juice of 2 lemons
8 sprigs fresh parsley	Salt and pepper to taste
4 whole trout	

Place 2 sprigs of rosemary, oregano and parsley in each trout cavity. Place trout in a glass baking dish. Whisk together oil and lemon juice and pour over fish. Season with salt and pepper. Cover and refrigerate 1 to 2 hours, turning once. When ready to cook, preheat grill. Remove trout and pour oil marinade into a small pan. Bring to a boil. Meanwhile, grill trout 15 to 20 minutes, turning once. Serve trout with marinade sauce on the side.

Yield: 4 servings

Cabin Bluff
Broiled Speckled Trout

¼ cup fresh lemon juice
1 tablespoon oil
½ teaspoon Worcestershire sauce

Dash of hot pepper sauce
1½ pounds trout fillets with skin on
Salt and pepper to taste

Combine lemon juice, oil, Worcestershire and hot pepper sauce. Place fillets, skin-side-up, on broiler pan. Brush with lemon juice mixture. Season with salt and pepper. Broil 3 to 4 inches from heat source until skin bubbles, about 4 minutes. Turn fillets, brush with marinade and sprinkle with salt and pepper. Broil until fish flakes easily with a fork, 6 to 8 minutes. Brush with remaining marinade and serve immediately.

Panhandle Pan-Fried Trout

½ cup white cornmeal
½ teaspoon freshly ground black pepper
½ cup chopped fresh parsley

2 (5- to 6-ounce) trout fillets, rinsed and patted dry
Canola oil

Combine cornmeal, pepper and parsley. Roll trout fillets in mixture, pressing mixture into fillets. Fry trout in oil over medium heat, turning once, until lightly browned, crisp and firm to the touch.

Yield: 2 servings

Savannah Flounder with Capers and Sun-Dried Tomato Sauce

Capers and Sun-Dried Tomato Sauce

1 cup heavy cream	4 plum tomatoes, diced
4 tablespoons butter	2 tablespoons chopped fresh parsley
¼ cup chopped sun-dried tomatoes	2 tablespoons capers

Flounder

4 (8-ounce) fillets	½ cup flour
Salt and pepper to taste	¾ cup vegetable oil

Bring cream to a boil and reduce by half. Reduce temperature and whisk in butter until melted. Add all tomatoes, parsley and capers. To prepare flounder, sprinkle fillets evenly with salt and pepper. Dredge fillets in flour. Sauté fillets in hot oil for 3 to 5 minutes on each side. Remove fish and drain on paper towels. Serve sauce over fillets.

Yield: 4 servings

Flounder with Fresh Spinach

2 large onions, diced	Juice of 1 lemon
1 stick butter, divided	4 (6- to 8-ounce) flounder fillets
2 pounds fresh spinach, washed and stemmed	½ cup dry white wine
1 teaspoon salt	½ cup chicken stock
1 teaspoon black pepper	Fresh parsley sprigs for garnish

Sauté onion in 4 tablespoons butter. Add spinach and bring to a boil. Cover, reduce heat and cook 5 minutes or until tender. Drain spinach. Stir in salt, pepper and lemon juice. Set aside and keep warm. Melt remaining 4 tablespoons butter in a sauté pan over medium heat. Add flounder fillets, wine and stock. Cook about 5 minutes on each side or until done. Serve flounder over spinach mixture. Garnish with parsley sprigs.

Yield: 4 servings

Flounder with Dijon Mustard Sauce

4	(8-ounce) flounder fillets	2	tablespoons diced shallots
	Salt and pepper to taste	1	cup heavy cream
¼	cup melted butter	2	tablespoons Dijon mustard
1	cup dry white wine	4	tablespoons butter

Preheat oven to 450°. Sprinkle flounder fillets with salt and pepper. Place fillets in a greased baking dish. Brush fillets with melted butter. Bake 5 to 8 minutes or until flaky. Meanwhile, combine wine and shallots in a saucepan. Bring to a boil and cook until wine is almost evaporated. Add cream and mustard. Season with salt and pepper. Bring to a boil and cook to reduce sauce. Whisk in 4 tablespoons butter. Serve sauce over flounder.

Yield: 4 servings

Spicy Baked Flounder

4	(6- to 8-ounce) flounder fillets	2	teaspoons minced garlic
	Salt and pepper to taste	1	tablespoon Dijon mustard
¼	cup mayonnaise	½	teaspoon cayenne pepper
	Juice of 1 lemon		

Preheat oven to 450°. Place fillets in a baking dish and season with salt and pepper. Combine mayonnaise, lemon juice, garlic, mustard and cayenne pepper in a bowl. Season with salt and pepper. Spread mixture over fillets. Bake for 15 to 20 minutes or until done.

Yield: 4 servings

Cumberland Baked Redfish

1 cup chopped green onion	Salt and pepper to taste
1 cup chopped celery	¼ cup chopped fresh parsley
1½ cups sliced fresh mushrooms	1 cup white wine
Olive oil for sautéing	Juice of 1 lemon
6 (6- to 8-ounce) redfish fillets	

Preheat oven to 400°. In a sauté pan, sauté onion, celery and mushrooms in olive oil. Place fillets in a greased baking pan. Season with salt and pepper. Spread sautéed vegetables over fillets. Sprinkle parsley on top. Add wine and lemon juice to pan. Bake 15 to 20 minutes, basting occasionally.

Yield: 6 servings

Low Country Baked Redfish

2 tablespoons olive oil	2 tablespoons butter
4 (6- to 8-ounce) redfish fillets	4 Roma tomatoes, chopped
1 onion, chopped	2 teaspoons capers
1 tablespoon minced garlic	Salt and pepper to taste
8 ounces fresh mushrooms, chopped	

Preheat oven to 325°. Pour olive oil in a baking pan. Add fillets and bake 5 to 6 minutes. In a sauté pan, sauté onion, garlic and mushrooms in butter for about 3 minutes. Add tomatoes and capers. Season with salt and pepper and cook 3 minutes longer. Spoon vegetables over fish and bake 5 minutes longer or until fish is done.

Yield: 4 servings

Spicy Redfish

4   (8-ounce) redfish fillets
    Salt and pepper to taste
    Hot pepper sauce to taste
¼   cup vegetable oil
1   green bell pepper, sliced

1   red bell pepper, sliced
2   tablespoons minced garlic
1   onion, chopped
3   tablespoons olive oil

Season fillets with salt, pepper and pepper sauce. In a large skillet, sauté fillets in vegetable oil over medium heat for 5 to 6 minutes on each side. Meanwhile, sauté bell peppers, garlic and onion in olive oil in a medium sauté pan until vegetables are tender. Serve vegetables over fish.

Yield: 4 servings

Golden Baked Spanish Mackerel

2   teaspoon salt
¾   cup milk
4   (6- to 8-ounce) mackerel fillets

2   cups slightly crushed cornflakes
¼   cup melted butter

Preheat oven to 425°. Dissolve salt in milk. Dip fillets in milk mixture, then roll in cornflake crumbs. Place fillets in a greased baking pan. Pour butter over fillets. Bake about 20 minutes.

Yield: 4 servings

Poached Redfish with Dill

4   redfish fillets
¼   cup white vinegar
1   onion, sliced
6   sprigs dill weed

¼   teaspoon cayenne pepper
     Salt to taste
10   whole black peppercorns

Place fillets in a large skillet. Add vinegar, onion, dill, cayenne pepper, salt and peppercorns. Add enough cold water to cover fillets. Bring to a boil. Reduce heat to a simmer and cook 5 to 6 minutes or until done. Remove fillets and serve with your favorite sauce.

Yield: 4 servings

Harbour Island Redfish

1   green bell pepper, cubed
1   red bell pepper, cubed
1   tablespoon minced garlic
1   medium onion, chopped

¼   cup olive oil
1½   pounds redfish fillets, cut into
       1-inch cubes
     Hot pepper sauce to taste

Sauté bell peppers, garlic and onion in oil in a skillet for 6 minutes over medium heat. Add fish and stir well to coat. Cover and cook 7 to 8 minutes. Stir and season with hot sauce. Cook 5 minutes longer. Serve over jasmine rice.

Yield: 4 servings

Sanibel Pan-Fried Snook

6	(6- to 8-ounce) snook fillets		Salt and pepper to taste
½	cup milk	½	cup vegetable oil
½	cup all-purpose flour		

Place snook fillets in a dish. Pour milk over fish; turn once. Combine flour, salt and pepper in a flat dish. Remove fillets from milk and dredge in seasoned flour until coated well. Shake off excess flour. Heat oil in a sauté pan over medium-high heat. Add fillets and cook 4 to 6 minutes on each side or until golden brown. Serve with a Caper Tartar Sauce (page 88) or your favorite sauce.

Yield: 6 servings

Grilled Black Tip Shark

½	cup olive oil	2	tablespoons minced garlic
	Juice of 1 lemon		Salt and pepper to taste
2	teaspoons chopped fresh basil	4	(8-ounce) shark steaks
2	teaspoons chopped fresh oregano		

Combine oil, lemon juice, basil, oregano, garlic, salt and pepper in a large bowl. Add shark steaks and refrigerate 1½ hours. When ready to cook, preheat grill. Remove steaks from marinade, reserving marinade. Place steaks on grill and cook 5 minutes on each side, basting frequently with marinade.

Yield: 4 servings

Grilled Bluefish with Tomato and Pesto

¼	cup olive oil, divided	½	tablespoon minced garlic
4	(6- to 8-ounce) bluefish fillets	1	large tomato, diced
	Salt and pepper to taste	½	cup store-bought pesto
1	large onion, diced	⅓	cup Parmesan cheese

Preheat grill. Rub 1 to 2 tablespoons of olive oil over fillets to coat. Season fillets with salt and pepper and grill for 12 to 15 minutes or until done. Meanwhile, sauté onion and garlic in remaining olive oil until tender. Add tomato and pesto and cook until heated through. Season to taste. Spoon sauce over fillets. Sprinkle with cheese.

Yield: 4 servings

Ocracoke Batter-Fried Bluefish

1	cup baking mix		Vegetable oil for frying
1	tablespoon Old Bay seasoning	2	pounds bluefish fillets, cut into
1	egg		strips
	Salt and pepper to taste		

Combine baking mix, Old Bay seasoning, egg, salt and pepper to make a batter. Heat oil in a deep fryer to about 375°. Dip fish strips in batter. Deep-fry strips in hot oil and drain on paper towels. Serve with dipping sauces.

Yield: 4 to 6 servings

Bluefish and New Potato Kebabs

16   small new potatoes
1½ pounds bluefish, cubed
¼   cup olive oil

2   tablespoons sweet paprika
    Salt and pepper to taste

Cook potatoes until tender, drain and cool. Cut potatoes in half. Combine potatoes and remaining ingredients in a large bowl. Cover and refrigerate for about 2 hours. When ready to cook, preheat grill. Using 8 to 10 skewers, prepare kebabs by alternating potatoes and fish. Grill kebabs 8 to 10 minutes, turning occasionally. Serve with tartar sauce.

Yield: 4 to 6 servings

Seared Bluefish with Wasabi Butter

Bluefish
¼   cup soy sauce
1   tablespoon chopped fresh cilantro
1   tablespoon sesame oil
    Juice of ½ lemon

1½ tablespoons minced ginger
1   tablespoon minced garlic
4   (8-ounce) bluefish fillets
4   tablespoons butter

Wasabi Butter
4   tablespoons butter
    Juice of ½ lemon

½   teaspoon powdered wasabi

Combine soy sauce, cilantro, oil, lemon juice, ginger and garlic in a bowl. Add fillets and marinate for about 1 hour. Melt butter in a sauté pan over high heat. Add fillets and sear 4 minutes on both sides or to desired doneness, basting occasionally with marinade. To prepare Wasabi Butter, combine butter, lemon juice and wasabi. Mix until smooth. Serve with fillets.

Yield: 4 servings

Market Favorites

Grouper over Basil Mashed Potatoes with Roasted Pepper Pesto

Roasted Pepper Pesto

4   ounces fresh basil
4   red bell peppers, roasted, peeled and seeded
8   cloves garlic
¼   cup Parmesan cheese

Dash of cayenne pepper
2   tablespoons pine nuts, toasted
Salt and pepper to taste
Extra virgin olive oil

Basil Mashed Potatoes

2   cups mashed potatoes

2   large basil leaves, finely chopped

Grouper

4   (7-ounce) grouper steaks
    Oil for searing

4   teaspoons butter

To make pesto, combine basil, bell pepper, garlic, cheese, cayenne pepper and pine nuts in a food processor or blender. Season with salt and pepper. Add olive oil to form a soft paste consistency. Prepare potatoes by combining hot mashed potatoes with chopped basil. To make the grouper, sear fish in oil over high heat for 1 minute. Turn fish and place 1 teaspoon butter on each steak. Transfer to oven and bake at 400° for 5 to 6 minutes. To serve, divide mashed potatoes among 4 plates. Place grouper over potatoes and top with a dollop of pesto.

Yield: 4 servings

Grouper with Sautéed Mushrooms and Crabmeat

3	eggs, beaten		Salt and pepper to taste
2	tablespoons water	8	ounces mushrooms, sliced
3	tablespoons butter, divided	1	cup heavy cream
4	(8-ounce) grouper fillets	2	tablespoons dry sherry
½	cup flour	4	ounces crabmeat

Combine egg and water in a flat dish. Heat 1½ tablespoons butter in a skillet. Dredge fillets in flour, then dip in egg wash and sauté until golden brown and done. Season with salt and pepper. In a separate pan, sauté mushrooms in remaining 1½ tablespoons butter. Sprinkle over fish. Add cream, sherry and crabmeat to same pan and bring to a boil. Season to taste. Pour sauce over fish.

Yield: 4 servings

Grouper Amandine

¼	cup all-purpose flour		Salt and pepper to taste
1	cup sliced almonds, divided	4	tablespoons butter, divided
4	(6- to 8-ounce) grouper fillets	½	cup dry white wine

Blend flour and ½ cup almonds in a food processor until fine. Pour mixture into a bowl. Season grouper fillets with salt and pepper. Dredge fillets in flour mixture to coat. In a large skillet, sauté remaining ½ cup almonds in 1 to 2 tablespoons of butter until golden. Remove from pan and set aside. Add remaining butter to skillet and add fillets. Sauté fish about 5 minutes on each side. Transfer fish to a serving platter and keep warm. Add wine to skillet and whisk over medium heat until sauce simmers. Season sauce with salt and pepper. Spoon sauce over fish. Sprinkle toasted almonds on top.

Yield: 4 servings

Pistachio Crusted Snapper with Gorgonzola Cream

Snapper

3	cups breadcrumbs	½	tablespoon salt
1	cup chopped pistachio nuts	3	eggs, beaten
2	tablespoons finely chopped fresh thyme	2	cups milk
½	tablespoon black pepper	4-6	(7-ounce) snapper fillets
		1	cup olive oil

Sauce

1	small white onion, diced	1	tablespoon chopped garlic
½	tablespoon salt	½	tablespoon seafood base
	Black pepper to taste	3	cups heavy cream
¾	cup red wine	½	cup crumbled Gorgonzola cheese
2	tablespoons Worcestershire sauce	2	tablespoons chopped scallions

Combine breadcrumbs, nuts, thyme, pepper and salt in a shallow dish. Combine egg and milk in a separate dish for an egg wash. Dust snapper fillets with breadcrumb mixture, dip in egg wash, and then roll in seasoned flour. Sauté fillets in olive oil until golden brown. To prepare sauce, sauté onion in a skillet. Season with salt and pepper. Deglaze skillet with red wine. Add Worcestershire sauce, garlic and seafood base. Cook until reduced to ¼ cup. Add cream and reduce to desired consistency. Stir in cheese and scallions. Serve sauce over fillets.

Yield: 4 to 6 servings

Snapper Hemingway

Snapper

4   (8-ounce) snapper fillets
½   cup flour
    Juice of 1 lemon
    Salt to taste

½   cup sesame seeds
    Butter for sautéing
    Water or wine for baking

Lemon Blanc Sauce

1   cup heavy cream
6   tablespoons lemon juice

4   tablespoons butter, quartered

Dredge snapper in flour, then rub with lemon juice. Season with salt and dip in sesame seeds. Sauté in butter in a skillet until brown on one side. Add water or wine to cover bottom of skillet and bake at 450° for about 8 minutes. Meanwhile, prepare sauce by combining cream and lemon juice in a saucepan. Bring to a boil and reduce until thickened. Remove from heat, add butter and whisk until smooth. Transfer baked fish to individual plates. Pour sauce over fish and serve.

Yield: 4 servings

Salmon with Pineapple Salsa

Pineapple Salsa

1   (8-ounce) can crushed pineapple in its own juice
½   red bell pepper, minced
½   green bell pepper, minced
½   red onion, minced

¼   cup chopped fresh cilantro
    Juice of ½ lime
1   jalapeño pepper, seeded and minced
    Salt and pepper to taste

Salmon

4   (6- to 8-ounce) salmon steaks

1   tablespoon soy sauce

Combine all salsa ingredients in a bowl. Set aside. To prepare salmon, preheat broiler. Brush salmon with soy sauce and place in a broiler pan. Broil about 3 to 4 minutes on each side or until done.

Yield: 4 servings

Rice Stuffed Grouper

1 onion, diced	1 teaspoon dill weed
1 cup sliced mushrooms	1½ cups dry brown rice
1 tablespoon butter	1 cup grated carrot
1¼ cups chicken broth	4 (6-ounce) grouper fillets
¼ cup half-and-half	Salt and pepper to taste
1 tablespoon cornstarch	

Preheat oven to 350°. Sauté onion and mushrooms in butter. Add broth, half-and-half, cornstarch and dill weed. Bring to a boil. Add rice and return to a boil. Reduce heat and cover. Simmer 15 minutes. Remove from heat. Stir in carrot and let stand 5 minutes. Stuff grouper by wrapping each fillet around a mound of rice mixture. Place remaining rice around fish in a greased baking dish. Season with salt and pepper. Bake 15 to 20 minutes.

Yield: 4 servings

Fried Grouper with Spicy Tartar Sauce

Grouper

¾ cup all-purpose flour	4 (8-ounce) grouper fillets
¼ cup cornstarch	½ cup buttermilk
1 tablespoon garlic powder	Oil for frying
Salt and pepper to taste	

Spicy Tartar Sauce

1 cup mayonnaise	1 tablespoon capers
1 tablespoon sweet pickle relish	1 jalapeño pepper, seeded and minced
1 tablespoon dill pickle relish	

Combine flour, cornstarch, garlic, salt and pepper. Dredge fillets in flour mixture, then dip in buttermilk and dredge again in flour mixture. Heat oil in an electric frying pan to 350°. Fry grouper in oil for 5 to 8 minutes or until done. Drain on paper towels. To make tartar sauce, combine all ingredients. Cover and chill. Serve sauce with grouper.

Yield: 4 servings

Fried Shrimp and Gravy

1½ pounds shrimp, peeled and
    deveined
    Salt and pepper to taste
¾ cup flour
½ cup yellow cornmeal
½ cup olive oil, divided
1 onion, diced

1 red bell pepper, diced
1 green bell pepper, diced
1 tablespoon chopped garlic
1 cup chopped tasso
4 cups broth
    Hot pepper sauce to taste

Season shrimp with salt and pepper. Dust with flour and cornmeal, shaking off excess. Reserve flour for later use. Heat oil in a skillet. Add shrimp and sauté until vegetables are tender. Dust vegetables with reserved flour. Stir in broth and cook to make a thick sauce. Add shrimp and cook 1 minute. Season with salt, pepper and hot pepper sauce. Serve with rice or polenta.

Yield: 4 servings

Linguine with Crab and Mushrooms

1 (8-ounce) bottle clam juice
1 teaspoon saffron threads
4 tablespoons butter
1 pound fresh shiitake mushrooms,
    sliced
    Salt and pepper to taste
1 cup thinly sliced green onion

2 tablespoons tomato paste
½ tablespoon minced garlic
12 ounces lump crabmeat
1 tablespoon fresh tarragon
1 pound dry linguine, cooked al
    dente

Combine clam juice and saffron threads in a small bowl. Melt butter in a heavy sauté pan over medium heat. Add mushrooms and sauté about 2 minutes. Season with salt and pepper. Mix in green onion, tomato paste and garlic. Add clam juice mixture and bring to a simmer. Stir in crab and tarragon and cook until heated through. Season with salt and pepper. Add cooked linguine and toss to coat.

Yield: 4 servings

Poached Salmon Chambord

2	cups Chardonnay or dry white wine	1	tablespoon fresh lemon juice
4	cups water	1	teaspoon kosher salt
½	teaspoon black peppercorns	¾	cup Merlot or Zinfandel
	Dill to taste	¼	cup Chambord liqueur
	Thyme to taste	1	teaspoon cornstarch
	Fennel seed to taste	¾	cup sliced shiitake mushrooms
4	(6- to 8-ounce) salmon fillets		Kosher salt and freshly ground pepper to taste

Place Chardonnay, water, peppercorns, dill, thyme and fennel in a large baking pan. Bring to a boil over medium heat. Simmer 3 minutes. Meanwhile, rub fillets with lemon juice and sprinkle with salt. Let stand 2 minutes and then transfer fillets, in a single layer, to baking pan. Return Chardonnay broth to a simmer and cook 3 minutes per inch fillet thickness. Do not allow broth to boil rapidly. Meanwhile, add Merlot to a saucepan over medium heat. In a separate container, whisk together Chambord and cornstarch until smooth. Add to Merlot and whisk constantly until thickened and smooth. Season mushrooms with salt and pepper and sauté in a skillet. To serve, pour Merlot sauce onto a platter. Arrange fillets on platter and top with mushrooms.

Yield: 4 servings

Boiled Blue Crabs

½	cup Old Bay seasoning	2	bay leaves
1	lemon, halved	1	dozen fresh crabs
	Dash of hot pepper sauce		

Fill a large pot half full with water. Bring to a boil. Add Old Bay seasoning, lemon, hot pepper sauce and bay leaves. Add crab and cook until red. Serve with melted butter and cocktail sauce.

Cilantro Crab Salad

¼	cup finely chopped red onion	1	teaspoon fresh lime juice
¼	cup mayonnaise	8	ounces crabmeat
2	tablespoons chopped fresh cilantro		Salt and pepper to taste

Combine onion, mayonnaise, cilantro and lime juice in a bowl. Mix in crabmeat. Season with salt and pepper. Serve on a bed of greens.

Yield: 2 to 4 servings

Grilled Scallops with Mango Sauce

Scallops

24	large sea scallops	1	teaspoon kosher salt
½	cup olive oil		Black pepper to taste

Mango Sauce

2	medium mangoes, chopped		Juice of 1 lime
2	small cucumbers, peeled, seeded and chopped	2	tablespoons balsamic vinegar
¼	cup olive oil	¼	teaspoon curry powder
			Salt and pepper to taste

Preheat grill to high heat. Brush scallops with oil. Sprinkle with salt and pepper. Grill scallops 4 to 5 minutes, turning once. Serve warm with sauce. To make Mango Sauce, combine all ingredients in a food processor. Process until smooth, scraping down sides once.

Yield: 4 servings, 2 cups sauce

Rice Fried Giant Sea Scallops with Jalapeño Tomato Coulis

Jalapeño Tomato Coulis

2	jalapeño peppers, roasted and seeded	½	teaspoon cayenne pepper
10	plum tomatoes, roasted and peeled	½	teaspoon chili powder
½	small white onion	1	tablespoon salt
2	teaspoons ground cumin	½	tablespoon pepper
		4	cups tomato juice
		¼	cup vinegar

Sea Scallops

1¼	pounds giant sea scallops	8	egg yolks, beaten
1½	cups flour	5	cups cooked white rice
	Salt and pepper to taste		

Combine all coulis ingredients in a blender or food processor and puree. When ready to serve, dust scallops in flour seasoned with salt and pepper. Dip in egg yolk and then coat with rice. Deep-fry at 375° until golden brown. Serve with coulis.

Yield: 4 to 6 servings

Mediterranean-Style Salmon

	Olive oil for sautéing		Salt and pepper to taste
1	onion, chopped	4	(6- to 8-ounce) salmon fillets
1	(14½-ounce) can diced tomatoes in juice	½	cup white wine
1	tablespoon oregano	¼	cup halved black olives
		½	cup crumbled feta cheese

Preheat oven to 425°. Heat oil in a sauté pan. Add onion and sauté until tender. Add tomatoes, oregano, salt and pepper. Cook 10 to 15 minutes. Place fillets in a baking dish. Add wine. Cover with tomato mixture. Add olives and cheese. Bake 20 to 30 minutes or until done.

Yield: 4 servings

Grilled Salmon with Spicy Chili Butter

Grilled Salmon

4	(6- to 8-ounce) salmon fillets	Juice of ½ lemon
¼	cup olive oil	Salt and pepper to taste

Spicy Chili Butter

1	stick butter	2 tablespoons minced and seeded
¼	cup minced shallots	jalapeño pepper
		Salt and pepper to taste

Preheat grill. Coat fillets with oil, lemon juice, salt and pepper. Grill 8 to 10 minutes, turning once. To prepare Spicy Chili Butter, combine butter, shallots, jalapeño pepper, salt and pepper in a small bowl. Mix well and spoon onto plastic wrap. Roll plastic into a cylinder and chill for 2 to 3 hours. Serve with salmon fillets.

Yield: 4 servings

Salmon Piccata

1½	pounds salmon fillets	1	cup dry white wine
1	cup bread crumbs	2	tablespoons lemon juice
½	cup grated Parmesan cheese	4	tablespoons butter
	Butter for sautéing	2	tablespoons capers
1	shallot, minced	½	cup shredded Parmesan cheese
1½	tablespoons olive oil		Salt and pepper to taste

Slice salmon into ½-inch thick fillets. Combine bread crumbs and grated Parmesan cheese in a flat dish. Dredge fillets in crumb mixture to coat. Sauté in butter 2 to 3 minutes on both sides. Transfer fillets to a serving platter and keep warm. In a sauté pan, sauté shallot in olive oil. Add wine and lemon juice and cook to reduce. Whisk in 4 tablespoons butter until melted. Add capers. Pour sauce over fish. Sprinkle with shredded Parmesan cheese.

Yield: 4 to 6 servings

Enon Plantation Salmon Patties

2	eggs, lightly beaten	¼	cup flour
1	(15-ounce) can pink salmon, rinsed and drained	¼	cup cornmeal
		5	crackers, crushed
⅓	cup onion, chopped		Pepper

Combine eggs, salmon and onion. Mix flour, cornmeal, cracker crumbs and pepper. Add to salmon mixture. Form into patties and fry until golden brown.

Yield: 4 servings

Cabin Bluff Shrimp Creole

1½ pounds fresh shrimp in shells
2 tablespoons olive or canola oil
½ cup celery, coarsely chopped
½ cup onion, coarsely chopped
½ cup green bell pepper, coarsely chopped
2 cups tomatoes, chopped

2 tablespoons parsley, minced
½ teaspoon paprika
1 large bay leaf
⅛ teaspoon crushed red pepper
⅛ teaspoon dried thyme, crumbled
½ teaspoon hot pepper sauce
Salt and pepper

Bring a large pot of salted water to a boil. Add shrimp and return to a boil. Reduce heat and simmer until shrimp turn pink, 2 to 3 minutes. Drain, peel and devein. Heat oil in a 2-quart saucepan. Sauté celery, onion and bell pepper until tender but not brown. Add tomatoes, parsley, paprika, bay leaf, red pepper, thyme and hot pepper sauce. Simmer, uncovered, until the desired consistency, 10 to 15 minutes. Discard bay leaf. Add shrimp to sauce and heat just until hot. Season to taste with salt and pepper.

Yield: 3 to 4 servings

Romano Crusted Shrimp

Sun-Dried Tomato and Basil Cream Sauce

5   cups heavy cream
¾   cup julienne sun-dried tomato
¼   cup julienne fresh basil

1   teaspoon chicken base
     Salt and pepper to taste

Shrimp

2   pounds (16/20 count) shrimp,
        peeled and deveined
     Flour for dusting
     Salt and pepper to taste
2½   cups Romano cheese

2½   cups bread crumbs
3   eggs, beaten
2   cups milk
     Angel hair pasta, cooked al dente

Combine cream, tomato, basil and chicken base in a saucepan. Season with salt and pepper. Cook until reduced to desired consistency. To prepare shrimp, dust shrimp in flour seasoned with salt and pepper. Combine cheese and bread crumbs in a shallow dish. In separate bowl, combine eggs, milk and dip shrimp in egg wash, then coat with breadcrumb mixture. Deep-fry 6 to 8 minutes. Serve over angel hair pasta and top with cream sauce.

Shrimp and Scallop Alfredo

1   pound shrimp, peeled and
        deveined
1   pound scallops
4   tablespoons butter
2   cups heavy cream
1   red bell pepper, thinly sliced

½   cup grated Parmesan cheese
2   teaspoons chopped garlic
1   (16-ounce) package pasta, cooked
        al dente
     Salt and pepper to taste
½   cup shredded Parmesan cheese

In a large skillet, sauté shrimp and scallops in butter over medium heat until light pink. Stir in cream and simmer until bubbly. Add bell pepper, grated Parmesan cheese, garlic and pasta. Toss gently and season with salt and pepper. Sprinkle with shredded Parmesan cheese and serve.

Yield: 4 servings

Shrimp and Scallop Curry

3 tablespoons butter
1 tablespoon minced ginger
2 tablespoons minced garlic
½ tablespoon curry powder
1 pound large shrimp
½ pound sea scallops

½ cup sliced red bell pepper
½ cup chopped green onion
1½ cups heavy cream
Salt and pepper to taste
1 cup dry jasmine rice, cooked

Melt butter in a sauté pan over medium heat. Add ginger and garlic and sauté about 3 minutes. Add curry, shrimp, scallops, bell pepper and onion. Sauté until shrimp are pink. Add cream and simmer 5 minutes or until sauce thickens slightly. Season with salt and pepper. Serve with cooked rice.

Yield: 4 servings

Crab Cakes

1 pound fresh crabmeat
½ red bell pepper, chopped
½ cup chopped green onion
1 tablespoon lemon juice
¼ cup mayonnaise
2 teaspoons Dijon mustard
1 tablespoon Old Bay seasoning

Hot pepper sauce to taste
Salt and pepper to taste
1 egg
½ package or more saltine crackers, crushed, divided
¼ cup olive oil

Combine crabmeat, bell pepper, onion, lemon juice, mayonnaise, mustard, Old Bay seasoning and hot pepper sauce in a large bowl. Season with salt and pepper. Mix in egg and half the cracker crumbs. Shape crab mixture into patties. Place remaining cracker crumbs in a dish. Dredge patties in crumbs to coat. Heat oil in a large sauté pan. Add patties and cook 4 minutes on each side or until golden brown. Serve with your favorite sauce.

Yield: 6 servings

Cabin Bluff
Crab Cakes with Dill Sauce

1 green onion, finely chopped	1 egg, lightly beaten
1 clove garlic, pressed	½ teaspoon parsley, minced
2 tablespoons red bell pepper, finely chopped	1 cup bread crumbs, divided
1 tablespoon butter	1 pound fresh white or claw crab meat, picked through for shells
Cayenne pepper	¼ cup Parmesan cheese, grated
3 tablespoons whipping cream	2 tablespoons olive oil
1 tablespoon Dijon mustard	2 tablespoons butter

Sauté onion, garlic and bell pepper in butter until onion is translucent. Remove form heat and add cayenne, cream and mustard. Stir in egg, parsley and ½ cup bread crumbs. Blend well. Gently mix in crab meat. Divide mixture into eight ½-inch thick patties. Combine remaining bread crumbs and Parmesan cheese. Press lightly on both sides of the cakes. Cover and refrigerate until firm, about 2 hours. Place on a greased baking sheet and drizzle with oil and butter. Bake in a preheated 400 degree oven 7 to 10 minutes. Serve with Dill Sauce.

Dill Sauce

1 cup mayonnaise	2 teaspoons lemon juice
¼ cup buttermilk	1 tablespoon grated lemon rind
2 tablespoons chopped fresh dill	1 clove garlic, minced
1 tablespoon minced fresh parsley	

Combine all ingredients and chill until mixture thickens. Garnish each crab cake with a spoonful.

Sauté Soft Shell Crabs with Lemon Butter Sauce

Crabs

2	eggs		Salt and pepper to taste	
1	cup milk	8	medium soft shell crabs	
1	cup flour	¼	cup oil	
1	tablespoon Old Bay seasoning	4	tablespoons butter	

Lemon Butter Sauce

1	cup heavy cream		Salt to taste
	Juice of 1 lemon		Chopped parsley
1	stick butter		

Beat eggs and milk together. Combine flour, Old Bay seasoning, salt and pepper in a shallow pan. Soak crabs in egg mixture for about 2 minutes. Dip in flour mixture. Combine oil and butter in a skillet over medium heat. Add crabs and sauté until golden brown on both sides. Serve with Lemon Butter Sauce. To make sauce, bring cream to a boil in a saucepan. Remove from heat and whip in lemon juice, butter, salt and parsley.

Yield: 4 servings

Low Country Boil

½	cup Old Bay seasoning	2	pounds kielbasa sausage
½	cup lemon	3	pounds medium to large shrimp in their shells
12-16	new potatoes		
8	small onions		Salt and pepper to taste
6	ears of corn, halved		

Fill a 12-quart pot half full with water. Bring to a boil. Add Old Bay seasoning and lemon. Add potatoes and onions and boil 10 minutes. Add corn and sausage and boil 10 minutes longer. Reduce heat to a simmer and add shrimp. Cook until shrimp are done and potatoes are tender. Season with salt and pepper. Serve with melted butter and cocktail sauce.

Yield: 6 to 8 servings

Linguine with Spicy Clam Sauce

¼ cup olive oil	¾ cup heavy cream
1 large onion, chopped	1 pound dry linguine, cooked al
1½ tablespoons minced garlic	dente
1 tablespoon dried red pepper flakes	½ cup chopped fresh basil
1 teaspoon oregano	Salt and pepper to taste
4 (6½-ounce) cans chopped clams with liquid	

Heat oil in a large skillet over medium heat. Add onion, garlic, pepper flakes and oregano. Sauté until onion is tender. Add clams and cream. Simmer until slightly thickened. Add cooked linguine and basil and toss until coated. Season with salt and pepper.

Yield: 4 servings

Pasta with Clams

2 tablespoons olive oil	2 cups white wine
¼ cup chopped garlic	½ cup chopped parsley
Salt and pepper to taste	1 pound asparagus, diced
2 (10-ounce) cans minced clams with juice	10 plum tomatoes, chopped
1 (2¼-ounce) can sliced black olives	½ cup Romano cheese
	1 pound dry vermicelli, cooked al dente
Juice of 2 lemons	

Heat oil in a large skillet. Add garlic, salt, pepper and clams. Sauté 3 minutes. Add olives, lemon juice, wine, parsley, asparagus and plums. Cook 6 to 8 minutes. Stir in cheese and cooked vermicelli. Mix well and serve.

Yield: 4 servings

Chargrilled Swordfish with Roasted Pepper Salsa

Swordfish
4   (8-ounce) swordfish steaks
2   tablespoons olive oil

Salt and pepper to taste

Roasted Pepper Salsa
3   red bell peppers
2   tablespoons minced garlic
12 basil leaves, chopped

2   tablespoons red wine vinegar
¼   cup olive oil
Salt and pepper to taste

Preheat grill to medium heat. Brush steaks on both sides with oil. Grill steaks about 4 minutes on each side. Season with salt and pepper. To make salsa, grill and peel bell peppers. Seed and finely dice and place in a mixing bowl. Add garlic, basil, vinegar and oil. Season with salt and pepper. Cover and let stand 1 hour at room temperature. Spoon salsa over grilled steaks.

Yield: 4 servings

Seafood Pasta

¼   cup olive oil
¼   cup minced garlic
1   (14½-ounce) can diced tomatoes
½   tablespoon dried red pepper flakes
1½ cups white wine
    Salt and pepper to taste
½   pound scallops

½   pound shrimp
    Juice of 1 lemon
4   tablespoons butter
1   pound dry spaghetti, cooked al dente
¼   cup chopped parsley

Heat oil in a large skillet. Add garlic and sauté about 2 to 3 minutes. Add tomatoes, pepper flakes, wine, salt and pepper. Cook 5 minutes. Stir in scallops, shrimp, lemon juice and butter. Cook over high heat until seafood is done. Add cooked spaghetti and toss. Mix in parsley.

Yield: 6 servings

NOTES

On the Side
& Sauces

Cabin Bluff Wild Rice

1	cup wild rice	4	slices bacon or 2 slices thick-sliced bacon
4	cups water		
½	teaspoon salt	1	medium onion, sliced

Place rice in a strainer and wash thoroughly under running water. Combine rice, water and salt in a large saucepan. Bring to a boil, reduce heat, cover and boil gently until rice is nearly tender, about 40 minutes. Do not overcook. Drain rice in a colander and let stand 1 hour. Cook bacon in a large skillet until crisp. Drain, crumble and set aside. Reserve 1 tablespoon bacon drippings and discard the rest. Sauté onion in reserved drippings until tender but not brown. Add rice and bacon to skillet. Cook over low heat, stirring occasionally, until rice is heated through and flavors are blended.

Yield: 3 to 4 servings

Cabin Bluff Zesty Lemon Sesame Broccoli

3	pounds broccoli	2	tablespoons sesame seeds, lightly toasted
2	tablespoons minced garlic		
⅔	cup fresh lemon juice		

Trim broccoli florets and cut into small pieces. Peel stems and slice into thin rounds. Steam broccoli in a vegetable steamer until it turns bright green and is slightly tender, about 4 minutes. Drain and place in a salad bowl. Combine garlic and lemon juice. Pour over broccoli and toss to coat. Sprinkle with sesame seeds. Serve immediately to preserve color.

Yield: 6 to 8 servings

Wynfield Plantation Crispy Buttermilk Fried Corn

¾ cup self-rising flour
¾ cup yellow cornmeal
1¼ cups buttermilk
   Pepper

2 cups or more corn kernels
   (4 large ears)
   Salt

Combine flour, cornmeal, buttermilk and pepper to taste. Add enough corn to make batter thick. Drop by teaspoonfuls into hot 1-inch-deep oil. Brown on both sides. Drain well and salt to taste.

Baked Tomatoes

4 tomatoes, cored and halved
1 stick butter, melted, divided
   Salt and pepper to taste

½ cup bread crumbs
½ cup Parmesan cheese
2 tablespoons dried Italian herbs

Place tomatoes in a baking dish, cut side up, and brush with some of melted butter. Season with salt and pepper. Sprinkle bread crumbs, cheese, and herbs on top. Drizzle with remaining butter. Bake at 425° until topping is lightly browned.

Yield: 4 servings

Grandpa Turner's Vinaigrette Slaw

8 slices bacon, diced
¾ cup apple cider vinegar
¼ cup water

1 small head cabbage, shredded
   Salt and pepper to taste
1 small onion, thinly sliced

Sauté bacon in a skillet until brown. Cool. Stir in vinegar and water. Season cabbage with salt and pepper. Combine cabbage, onion and vinegar mixture. Toss and serve.

Yield: 8 servings

Creamy Polenta

4 cups chicken broth	¾ cup medium-grain polenta
¼ cup diced sun-dried tomatoes	½ cup sour cream
1 clove garlic, pressed	½ cup Parmesan cheese
1 tablespoon dried Italian herbs	

Bring chicken broth to a boil in a saucepan. Add tomatoes, garlic, and herbs and boil for 1 minute. Whisk in polenta, stirring constantly, until smooth. Reduce to a simmer and cook 20 minutes, stirring frequently. Remove from heat and stir in sour cream and cheese.

Yield: 4 to 6 servings

Sweet Potatoes Anna

3-4 large sweet potatoes	1 cup grated Parmesan cheese
¾ cup melted butter	Salt and pepper
¼ cup granulated garlic	

Peel and thinly slice potatoes. Place a quarter of the potatoes in a baking dish which has been coated with nonstick spray. Pour a quarter of the butter over potatoes. Sprinkle with a quarter of the garlic and top with ½ cup cheese. Season with salt and pepper to taste. Repeat layering 3 times. Cover dish with foil and bake in a preheated 400° oven for 30 minutes. Remove foil and bake an additional 15 minutes.

Roasted Asparagus

2　pounds fresh asparagus
2　tablespoons olive oil

Salt and pepper

Cut ends off asparagus. Brush with olive oil and season with salt and pepper to taste. Place on a baking sheet. Roast in preheated 450° oven until lightly browned and tender.

Squash Casserole

1　large onion, chopped
2　tablespoons butter
4　cups cooked squash
1　cup grated carrots

1　can cream of chicken soup
½　cup sour cream
2　cups bread crumbs, divided
　　Salt and pepper

Preheat oven to 350°. Sauté onions in butter until tender. Stir in squash, carrots, soup, sour cream and 1 cup bread crumbs. Season to taste with salt and pepper. Cook 5 minutes, stirring. Transfer to a buttered casserole dish. Top with remaining bread crumbs. Bake for 25 to 30 minutes.

Fried Green Tomatoes

3-4 firm green tomatoes
　　Salt
1½ cups cornmeal

Black pepper to taste
½　cup vegetable oil

Slice tomatoes to desired thickness. Place slices in a single layer on a flat surface. Sprinkle with salt to remove liquid. Season cornmeal with pepper. Dip tomato slices in cornmeal mixture until coated. Fry slices in hot oil until golden brown.

Yield: 4 to 6 servings

Creamy Grits with Cheese

3	cups canned chicken broth	1	cup quick-cooking grits
2	cups whole milk	½	cup grated sharp cheddar cheese
	Salt and pepper to taste	1	cup grated pepper-Jack cheese

Combine broth, milk, salt and pepper in a medium saucepan. Bring to a boil. Reduce heat to low and slowly whisk in grits. Cook 25 minutes, stirring frequently, or until thickened. Stir in cheeses.

Yield: 6 servings

Hush Puppies

1	cup white cornmeal	⅓	cup milk
⅓	cup all-purpose flour	2	teaspoons vegetable oil
1	teaspoon dark brown sugar	1	egg
	Salt and pepper		

Combine cornmeal, flour and brown sugar. Season with salt and pepper to taste. Mix milk, oil and egg in a separate bowl. Pour into dry mixture. Blend, adding a little water if necessary, but leaving batter thick enough for a spoon to stand in. Fill a frying pan 1½ inches deep with oil. Heat over medium high heat. Drop batter by tablespoonfuls into hot oil. Cook until golden brown and floating. Drain well on paper towels.

Mooney's Sour Cream Cornbread

¾	cup yellow cornmeal	1	cup sour cream
¾	cup all-purpose flour	2	eggs, lightly beaten
1	teaspoon salt	½	cup vegetable oil
3	teaspoons baking powder		Butter, softened

Combine cornmeal, flour, salt and baking powder in a mixing bowl. Add sour cream, eggs and oil. Stir until well blended. Pour into a greased 9-inch square pan. Bake in a preheated 400° oven 25 to 30 minutes. Spread with butter while warm.

Yield: 6 servings

Pinway Plantation Artichoke and Spinach Casserole

3	(10-ounce) packages frozen chopped spinach	3	(8-ounce) packages cream cheese, softened
4	teaspoons butter	2	tablespoons milk
	Salt and pepper	1	tablespoon garlic powder
2	(6-ounce) jars marinated artichoke hearts, drained and marinade reserved	½	cup chopped onion
		¾	cup grated Parmesan cheese

Cook spinach according to package directions. Drain. Add butter and salt to taste. Moisten with a little of the reserved marinade. Arrange artichokes and remaining marinade in the bottom of a greased 1½-quart glass baking dish. Top with spinach. Combine cream cheese, milk, garlic powder and onion. Beat until smooth. Spread over spinach. Season with pepper to taste. Sprinkle with Parmesan. Cover and refrigerate for 24 hours. Bake in a preheated 375° oven for 40 minutes.

Yield: 8 servings

Mary Alice's Layered Salad

1 large jar mayonnaise	1 (10-ounce) package frozen peas, thawed
3 tablespoons sugar	
1 head Bibb lettuce	1 cup shredded cheddar cheese
	1 jar bacon bits

Combine mayonnaise and sugar in a bowl. Let stand while making salad. Tear lettuce into bite-size pieces. Layer lettuce and peas in a large salad bowl. Spread top with mayonnaise mixture. Sprinkle with cheese and bacon bits. Let stand 10 minutes before serving.

Yield: 6 servings

Pinway Plantation Almond Mandarin Orange Salad

½ head red leaf lettuce	1 cup Mandarin oranges, drained
1 cup sliced celery	1 cup slivered almonds, roasted and salted
2 green onions, chopped	
1 tablespoon minced parsley	

Dressing

½ teaspoon salt	2 tablespoons sugar
Dash of pepper	2 tablespoons tarragon vinegar
¼ teaspoon hot pepper sauce	¼ cup vegetable oil

Tear lettuce into bite-size pieces and place in a salad bowl. Add remaining salad ingredients. Toss lightly, cover and chill. For Dressing: combine all ingredients in a blender and puree until blended. When ready to serve, pour over salad and toss to coat.

Yield: 2 servings

Marinated Green Beans

1   pound green beans
1   cup sliced red onion
½   cup olive oil
1   tablespoon minced garlic

¼   cup apple cider vinegar
1   tablespoon chopped fresh parsley
1   tablespoon Dijon mustard
    Salt and pepper to taste

Cook beans in boiling water until just tender. Drain and plunge into ice water to stop cooking; drain again. Combine beans and onions. In a separate container, mix oil, garlic, vinegar, parsley, mustard, salt and pepper. Pour mixture over vegetables and toss well. Cover and chill.

Yield: 4 to 6 servings

Summer Squash Sauté

4   tablespoons butter
1   cup thinly sliced onion
2   tablespoons chopped garlic
1   pound yellow squash, sliced into
        ⅓-inch rounds

1   pound small zucchini, sliced into
        ⅓-inch rounds
    Salt and pepper to taste

Melt butter in a large skillet over medium-high heat. Add onion and garlic and sauté until tender. Add squash and zucchini. Sauté 8 to 10 minutes or until tender. Season with salt and pepper.

Yield: 4 servings

Mediterranean Salad

1	pound mozzarella cheese, cubed	¾	cup vinaigrette dressing of choice
2	large tomatoes, chopped	½	cup chopped fresh basil
1	red bell pepper, chopped		Salt and pepper to taste

Combine cheese, tomato, bell pepper, dressing, basil, salt and pepper in a large bowl. Mix well. Cover and chill 1 hour.

Yield: 4 servings

Mashed Potatoes with Corn

2	ears fresh corn	2	tablespoons butter
1	medium onion, chopped	2	pounds russet potatoes, peeled and halved
1	tablespoon minced garlic		
1	tablespoon olive oil		Salt and pepper to taste
¾	cup heavy cream		

Cut corn from cob. Sauté corn, onion and garlic in oil until tender. Add cream and butter and bring to a boil. Remove from heat and set aside. Cook potatoes in boiling salted water until tender. Drain well and place in a large mixing bowl. Mash potatoes until smooth. Stir in corn mixture. Season with salt and pepper.

Yield: 4 servings

Sea Salt Baked Potatoes

4 baking potatoes	¼ cup sea salt
¼ cup oil	

Preheat oven to 425°. Wash and dry potatoes well. Rub potatoes with oil and place on a baking dish. Sprinkle salt over top to coat. Pierce potatoes with a fork. Bake 1½ hours or until done.

Yield: 4 servings

Rémoulade

1 cup mayonnaise	2 tablespoons capers
¼ cup Dijon mustard	2 teaspoons paprika
2 tablespoons chopped cornichon	1 tablespoon tarragon

Combine all ingredients in a bowl and mix well.

Caper Tartar Sauce

½ cup mayonnaise	¼ cup chopped fresh parsley
1 tablespoon milk	¼ teaspoon dried dill weed
1½ teaspoons mustard	Salt and pepper to taste
1½ teaspoons chopped capers	

Stir all ingredients together. Cover and chill.

Aïoli

1½ tablespoons minced garlic
1 egg yolk
1½ tablespoons Dijon mustard

Salt and pepper to taste
1 cup olive oil

Crush garlic using a mortar and pestle. Combine crushed garlic, egg yolk, mustard, salt and pepper in a mixing bowl. Slowly add oil by beating vigorously with a wire whisk. Whisk until all oil is mixed in and mixture is smooth and thick.

Rauigote

¼ cup finely diced onion
¼ cup finely diced shallot
1 teaspoon minced garlic
3 tablespoons chopped capers
¼ cup chopped fresh parsley
1 tablespoon dried tarragon

2 tablespoons chopped fresh chives
1 tablespoon dried chervil
¼ cup red wine vinegar
1 cup olive oil
Salt and pepper to taste

In a mixing bowl, combine all ingredients except oil, salt and pepper. Slowly add oil by beating vigorously with a wire whisk. Season with salt and pepper.

Yield: 4 to 6 servings

Cucumber Dill Salad

1 large cucumber, thinly sliced
½ cup sour cream
2 tablespoons cider vinegar

½ red onion, thinly sliced
2 teaspoons dill weed
Salt and pepper to taste

Combine cucumber, sour cream, vinegar, onion, dill weed, salt and pepper in a mixing bowl. Mix well. Chill 1 hour before serving.

Cabin Bluff Mixed Salad with Ginger Vinaigrette

2 tablespoons fresh lemon juice	Mixed salad greens
¼ cup olive oil	Sliced green and red bell peppers
1 clove garlic, minced	
½ teaspoon salt	Sliced fresh pears
½ teaspoon sugar	Pine nuts
½ teaspoon grated lemon rind	Freshly grated Parmesan cheese
½ teaspoon grated fresh ginger	

Combine lemon juice, olive oil, garlic, salt, sugar, lemon rind and ginger in a covered container. Shake well to blend. Place greens in a salad bowl and top with bell pepper slices, pears and pine nuts. Pour vinaigrette over salad and toss to coat. Garnish with Parmesan.

Cakes ~ Sweets ~ Pies ~ Cakes ~ Sweets ~ Pies ~ Cakes ~ Sweets ~ Pies ~ Ca
Sweets ~ Pies ~ Cakes ~ Sweets ~ Pies ~ Cakes ~ Sweets ~ Pies ~ Cakes ~ Sweets ~ F
Cakes ~ Sweets ~ Pies ~ Cakes ~ Sweets ~ Pies ~ Cakes ~ Sweets ~ Pies ~ Cakes ~ Swe
Pies ~ Cakes ~ Sweets ~ Pies ~ Cakes ~ Sweets ~ Pies ~ Cakes ~ Sweets ~ Pies ~ Ca
Sweets ~ Pies ~ Cakes ~ Sweets ~ Pies ~ Cakes ~ Sweets ~ Pies ~ Cakes ~ Sweets ~ F
Cakes ~ Sweets ~ Pies ~ Cakes ~ Sweets ~ Pies ~ Cakes ~ Sweets ~ Pies ~ Cakes ~ Swe
Pies ~ Cakes ~ Sweets ~ Pies ~ Cakes ~ Sweets ~ Pies ~ Cakes ~ Sweets ~ Pies ~ Ca

The Grand
Slam Finale

Sweets ~ Pies ~ Cakes ~ Pies ~ Cakes ~ Sweets ~ Pies ~ Cakes ~ Sweets ~ Pies ~ F
Cakes ~ Sweets ~ Pies ~ Cakes ~ Sweets ~ Pies ~ Cakes ~ Sweets ~ Pies ~ Cakes ~ Swe
Pies ~ Cakes ~ Sweets ~ Pies ~ Cakes ~ Sweets ~ Pies ~ Cakes ~ Sweets ~ Pies ~ Ca
Sweets ~ Pies ~ Cakes ~ Sweets ~ Pies ~ Cakes ~ Cakes ~ Sweets ~
Cakes ~ Sweets ~ Pies ~ Cakes ~ Swe ~ Cakes ~ Swe
Pies ~ Cakes ~ Sweets ~ Pies ~ Pies ~ Ca
Sweets ~ Pies ~ es ~ Sweets ~
Cakes ~ Sweets ~ Cakes ~ Swe
Pies ~ Cakes ~ Sweets ~ ~ Pies ~ Ca
Sweets ~ Pies ~ Cakes ~ Sweets ~
Cakes ~ Sweets ~ Pies ~ kes ~ Swe ~ Pies ~ Cakes ~ Swe
Pies ~ Cakes ~ Sweets ~ Pies ~ Cakes ~ Sweets ~ Pies ~ Cakes ~ Sweets ~ Pies ~ Ca
Sweets ~ Pies ~ Cakes ~ Sweets ~ Pies ~ Cakes ~ Sweets ~ Pies ~ Cakes ~ Sweets ~
Cakes ~ Sweets ~ Pies ~ Cakes ~ Sweets ~ Pies ~ Cakes ~ Sweets ~ Pies ~ Cakes ~ Sw
Pies ~ Cakes ~ Sweets ~ Pies ~ Cakes ~ Sweets ~ Pies ~ Cakes ~ Sweets ~ Pies ~ Ca
Sweets ~ Pies ~ Cakes ~ Sweets ~ Pies ~ Cakes ~ Sweets ~ Pies ~ Cakes ~ Sweets ~
Cakes ~ Sweets ~ Pies ~ Cakes ~ Sweets ~ Pies ~ Cakes ~ Sweets ~ Pies ~ Cakes ~ Sw
Pies ~ Cakes ~ Sweets ~ Pies ~ Cakes ~ Sweets ~ Pies ~ Cakes ~ Sweets ~ Pies ~ Ca
Sweets ~ Pies ~ Cakes ~ Sweets ~ Pies ~ Cakes ~ Sweets ~ Pies ~ Cakes ~ Sweets ~

Blueberry/Peach Pie

Crust

2	cups all-purpose flour
1	teaspoon salt
2	teaspoons light brown sugar
1/4	cup pecan meal

½ cup unsalted butter, chilled and
cut into small pieces
¼ cup ice water
1 egg white
Sugar

Filling

9 medium ripe peaches, peeled,
pitted and sliced
1 pint blueberries, picked over and
rinsed

1 cup firmly packed light brown
sugar
½ cup all-purpose flour

For Crust: Place flour, salt, brown sugar, pecan meal and butter in a mixing bowl with a paddle attachment. Mix until the dough resembles a coarse, dry meal. Add water at once and mix for 2 to 3 turns. Remove from bowl. Work the dough by hand until it forms a mass. Divide in half, shape into 2 disks, cover and refrigerate 30 minutes. Place each disk between sheets of wax paper and roll each into a circle about 12 inches in diameter. Place a disk in bottom of a 9-inch pie plate, overlapping 1 inch all around. Brush entire surface with egg white.

For Filling: Place peaches and blueberries in a bowl. Sprinkle with sugar and let stand 10 minutes. Add flour and mix until it is incorporated. Transfer filling to pie plate. Cover with remaining crust. Turn seams under and crimp together. Brush with egg white and sprinkle with sugar. Bake in a preheated 375° oven for 45 minutes.

Southern Baked Apples

6	Granny Smith apples	¼	cup brown sugar
1	teaspoon cinnamon	4	tablespoons butter
¾	teaspoon nutmeg	1	cup apple juice
½	cup sugar		

Preheat oven to 325°. Peel apples, core and cut in half vertically. Combine cinnamon, nutmeg and sugars. Sprinkle mixture over apple halves. Top with butter. Place apples in a baking dish. Pour juice into dish around apples. Bake 15 to 20 minutes or until tender. Serve with ice cream.

Yield: *4 to 6 servings*

Apple Plum Crisp

4	apples, peeled and sliced	1	teaspoon lemon juice
3	plums, sliced	1	cup dry quick oats
½	cup brown sugar	½	cup flour
½	cup granulated sugar	¼	teaspoon salt
2	teaspoons cinnamon	1½	sticks butter

Preheat oven to 375°. Combine apple and plum in a greased baking dish. Top with sugars, cinnamon and lemon juice. Combine oats, flour and salt in a bowl. Cut in butter. Sprinkle flour mixture over fruit. Bake 30 to 40 minutes.

Yield: *6 servings*

Strawberries with Champagne Sabayon

2   pints strawberries, stemmed,
    rinsed and drained
3   egg yolks
½   cup sugar

½   cup champagne
¼   cup Cointreau
    Pinch of sugar

Place 1½ inches of water in a saucepan and bring to a boil over high heat. Place egg yolks, ½ cup sugar and champagne in a stainless steel mixing bowl. Whisk to combine. Place bowl over boiling water and whisk constantly for 5 to 7 minutes or until thickened and glossy. Do not undercook. Remove from heat and whisk in Cointreau. Sprinkle strawberries with a pinch of sugar and toss. Arrange strawberries on a serving platter. Pour sauce in a small bowl for dipping.

Ruth's Sour Cream Pound Cake

1   cup butter, softened
3   cups sugar
1   cup sour cream
1   teaspoon vanilla
½   teaspoon lemon extract
½   teaspoon almond extract

3   cups cake flour
¼   teaspoon baking soda
¼   teaspoon baking powder
6   eggs
    Nutmeg

Cream butter and sugar until light and fluffy. Add sour cream and mix well. Add flavorings. Sift flour, baking soda and baking powder together. Add by thirds to butter mixture alternating with 2 eggs each time. Blend well after each addition. Pour into a greased tube pan and sprinkle with nutmeg. Bake in a preheated 325° oven until a tester inserted in center comes out clean, about 1 hour and 15 minutes.

Yield: 8 servings

Tiramisu Torte

Cake

1	teaspoon plus 2 tablespoons unsalted butter, melted, divided
2	teaspoons plus ½ cup flour, divided
3	eggs
3	egg yolks

½	cup granulated sugar
1	teaspoon vanilla
3	egg whites
3	tablespoons cornstarch

Icing and Topping

1	pound mascarpone cheese
8	ounces cream cheese
3	cups powdered sugar
3	ounces amaretto

3	ounces coffee liqueur
1	cup silvered almonds, toasted
¾	cup grated semisweet chocolate

Brush 1 teaspoon butter in a 9-inch cake pan. Dust pan with 2 teaspoons flour. Using an electric mixer, whip eggs, yolks and sugar at high speed for 5 minutes or until thickened and lemon colored. Add vanilla and whip 1 minute. Using a clean bowl and beaters, whip egg whites 2 minutes or until soft peaks form. Stir cornstarch and remaining flour into egg yolk batter. Gently fold into batter using a rubber spatula. Fold egg white and remaining butter into batter. Pour mixture into cake pan. Bake at 350° for 17 minutes. Remove from oven and cool 10 minutes. Turn out of pan and cool 30 minutes longer. To make icing, use an electric mixer to combine cheeses and sugar until smooth. To assemble torte, use a serrated knife to split cake in half, forming 2 circles. Drizzle halves with amaretto and liqueur. Frost the bottom layer of the torte. Place remaining layer on top and frost the top and sides. Press almonds onto the sides of the torte and sprinkle chocolate over the top.

Yield: 12 servings

Enon Plantation Chocolate Chip Cake

1   box yellow cake mix
1   small package instant vanilla
      pudding
1   cup vegetable oil
4   eggs
1   cup milk

1   bar German sweet
      chocolate, grated
1   cup chopped pecans
½   package semisweet
      chocolate morsels

Glaze

½   cup butter
3   tablespoons cocoa
5   tablespoons evaporated milk

1   box powdered sugar, sifted
1   teaspoon vanilla
1   cup chopped nuts

Combine cake mix, pudding, oil, eggs and milk in a large mixing bowl. Mix for 5 minutes. Stir in chocolate, nuts and morsels. Transfer to a greased and floured tube or Bundt pan. Bake in a preheated 325 degree oven for 55 minutes. Cover with foil and bake 15 minutes more. For Glaze: Place butter, cocoa and milk in a medium saucepan. Bring to a boil and remove from heat. Add sugar gradually, beating until smooth. Stir in vanilla and nuts. Pour over hot cake.

Pinway Plantation Amaretto Brownies

1	package brownie mix	3	eggs
½	cup vegetable oil	6	tablespoons amaretto

Filling

¾	cup butter, softened	3	tablespoons amaretto
2	cups powdered sugar		

Topping

6	ounces semisweet chocolate	4	tablespoons butter

Prepare brownie mix according to package directions, using oil and 3 eggs. Omit water. Turn into a 9 x 13-inch greased baking dish. Bake in a preheated 350° oven until done, about 25 to 30 minutes. Remove from oven and sprinkle with amaretto. Cool completely. For Filling: Combine all ingredients and beat until smooth. Spread over brownies and refrigerate at least 1 hour. For Topping: Place chocolate and butter in a small saucepan. Melt over low heat, stirring constantly. Spread over topping, cover and chill. Cut into squares to serve.

Yield: 12 servings

Park Avenue Squares

1	package butter cake mix	1	(8-ounce) package cream cheese, softened
½	cup butter, softened		
3	eggs	1	(16-ounce) package powdered sugar
1	cup chopped nuts		

Combine cake mix, butter, 1 egg and chopped nuts in a medium bowl. Press into a greased 9 x 13-inch baking dish. Lightly beat remaining 2 eggs in a medium bowl. Add cream cheese and combine well. Gradually add powdered sugar, beating until smooth. Spread over cake mixture. Bake in a preheated 350° oven for 30 to 40 minutes. Cut into squares to serve.

Yield: 8 servings

Southern Pecan Pie

3	eggs, lightly beaten	1	cup pecans
1	cup sugar	1	teaspoon vanilla
1	cup white corn syrup	1	unbaked pie crust
¼	cup butter, melted		

Combine eggs and sugar and mix thoroughly. Add syrup, butter, pecans and vanilla and blend well. Pour into pie crust. Bake in preheated 350° oven until a knife inserted in center comes out clean, 45 minutes to 1 hour.

Yield: 8 servings

Broiled Pineapple with Brown Sugar and Pecans

1	stick butter, melted	½	cup brown sugar
8	(½-inch thick) slices fresh pineapple, peeled	¼	cup chopped pecans

Preheat broiler. Brush some of melted butter in a baking dish. Arrange pineapple slices in dish. Sprinkle brown sugar over pineapple. Drizzle with remaining butter. Broil until pineapple is golden brown and bubbling. Sprinkle with pecans and broil 1 minute longer. Serve with your favorite ice cream.

Yield: 4 servings

Henderson Village Brownie Honey and Maple Syrup Cheesecake with Peanut Brittle Sauce

1 cup graham crackers, ground	2 tablespoons maple syrup
1 cup powdered sugar, divided	1 small package brownies, crushed
½ cup melted butter	1 cup whipping cream
1 pound cream cheese, softened	6 leaves gelatin
2 tablespoons honey, warmed	¼ cup cold water

Peanut Brittle Sauce

1 tablespoon molasses	¼ cup peanut brittle, finely ground
2 tablespoons hazelnut liqueur	8 ounces natural yogurt
¼ cup whipping cream	

Line bottom and sides of an 8-inch spring form pan with baking parchment. Combine graham cracker crumbs, ½ cup powdered sugar and butter. Press into bottom of pan and chill. Place cream cheese, honey, remaining ½ cup powdered sugar and brownies in a blender. Process for 1 minute. Add cream and mix 1 more minute. Put gelatin and water in a pan over low heat. Melt and add to cheese mixture when liquefied. Blend for 30 minutes. Pour into prepared crust and chill for 3 hours. For Sauce: Combine molasses and liqueur in a saucepan. Cook over low heat for a few minutes. Add cream and peanut brittle and cook for 5 minutes. Remove from heat and stir in yogurt. Serve over cheesecake.

Wynfield Plantation Chocolate Chunk Cookie Dough Cheesepie

Chocolate Crust

2½ cups crushed chocolate sandwich cookies, with filling

5 tablespoons butter, melted

Filling

2 (3-ounce) packages cream cheese, softened

⅓ cup sugar

⅓ cup sour cream

1 egg

½ teaspoon vanilla

Cookie Dough

2 tablespoons butter, softened

¼ cup firmly packed light brown sugar

¼ cup all-purpose flour

1 tablespoon water

¼ teaspoon vanilla

1 cup semisweet chocolate chunks or chips

For Crust: Preheat oven to 350 degrees. Finely grind cookies, including filling, in food processor. Combine with melted butter and press into bottom and up sides of a pie plate. For Filling: Place cream cheese and sugar in a small mixing bowl. Beat on medium speed until smooth. Blend in sour cream, egg and vanilla. Pour into prepared crust. For Cookie Dough: Beat butter and brown sugar in a small mixing bowl until light and fluffy. Add flour, water and vanilla and beat until blended. Stir in chocolate. Drop cookie dough by teaspoonfuls evenly onto cream cheese mixture. Bake until almost set in center, 35 to 40 minutes. Cool completely on a wire rack. Cover and refrigerate.

Yield: 8 servings

Cabin Bluff
Baked Apple Pudding
with Brandy Sauce

6	tablespoons butter, softened	¼	teaspoon salt
1	cup sugar	¼	teaspoon ground nutmeg
1	teaspoon vanilla	2	cups grated, unpeeled tart green apples
1	egg		
1	cup all-purpose flour	½	cup chopped pecans
1	teaspoon baking soda		

Place butter in a mixing bowl and beat on medium speed for 30 seconds. Add sugar and vanilla and mix until well blended. Add egg and beat for 1 minute. Combine flour, soda, salt and nutmeg. Add to butter mixture, beating on low speed until combined. Stir in apples and pecans. Turn mixture into a lightly greased 8-inch square baking pan. Bake in a preheated 350 degree oven until done, 40 to 45 minutes. Serve warm or cold with Brandy Sauce.

Yield: 8 to 10 servings

Cabin Bluff
Lemon Sugar Cookies

½	cup butter, softened	¼	teaspoon lemon extract
¼	cup vegetable shortening	1	egg, room temperature
1	cup sugar	2¼	cups all-purpose flour

Preheat oven to 375 degrees. Combine butter, shortening, sugar and lemon extract in a large mixing bowl until well-blended and fluffy. Add egg and beat well. Gradually add flour, beating on low speed after each addition until just moistened. Drop by rounded teaspoonfuls onto an ungreased cookie sheet. Press with fork tines to flatter. Bake until lightly browned, about 10 minutes.

Enon Plantation Bread Pudding

4	hot dog or hamburger buns	4	cups milk
8	eggs	2	tablespoons vanilla
3	cups sugar	1	cup margarine, melted

Preheat oven to 400 degrees. Place buns in a buttered 9 x 13-inch baking dish. Combine eggs and sugar, blending well. Add milk, vanilla and margarine. Pour over buns. Bake 30 minutes.

Yield: 8 servings

Enon Plantation Peach Cobbler

½	cup butter or margarine	¾	cup self-rising flour
1	cup sugar	1	large can peaches
1	cup evaporated milk		

Melt butter in a baking dish. Mix sugar, milk and flour in a medium bowl. Add butter. Stir in peaches and blend well. Return to baking dish. Bake in preheated 350 degree oven until brown, about 45 minutes.

Yield: 8 servings

NOTES

The Unlucky Fisherman

Rich-SeaPak Corporation is delighted to present a collection of winning recipes from the faculty chefs of Johnson & Wales University's College of Culinary Arts. Each year the chefs are challenged to create innovative recipes and menu concepts using SeaPak®'s seafood products found in your local grocery store or Food Clubs. Enjoy experimenting with some of the recipes created to make your dining table at home as much fun as your local seafood restaurant.

Rich-SeaPak Corporation was the first company to commercially bread, freeze and distribute shrimp in the world. Over fifty years later we are proud to continue to bring you quality seafood and non-seafood products made in two state-of-the-art plants in Brunswick, Georgia and Brownsville, Texas. You will find our seafood products in the freezer case under the SeaPak® brand; our non-seafood snack food and breakfast products are there too under the FarmRich® label. You can depend upon our products for quality, consistency and safety.

Schmitz's Garlic & Herb Shrimp Curry

1½	tablespoons olive oil	1	tablespoon fresh ginger, minced
19½	ounces SeaPak® Garlic Herb Marinated Shrimp	2	garlic cloves, minced
1½	ounces red bell pepper, seeded, cut into thin strips	1½	cups coconut milk
		4½	tablespoons fresh lime juice
1	tablespoon curry paste to taste	¾	cup cilantro, coarsely chopped
4	ounces snow peas, trimmed		Salt and pepper to taste

Heat half of the oil in a wok or sauté pan over high heat until it smokes. Add shrimp and red peppers. Stir-fry until shrimp appear opaque, about 2 minutes. Add curry paste, snow peas, ginger and garlic. Continue to cook about 2 minutes. Stir well to fully dissolve the curry paste. Add coconut milk to stir-fry mixture and bring to a simmer. Simmer until the sauce is slightly thickened and the peas are almost tender, about 3 minutes. Remove pan from heat. Stir in lime juice. Season to taste with salt and pepper. Serve with jasmine rice and garnish with cilantro.

Yield: 6 servings

Goellner's Greek Pita Pizza

2	tablespoons olive oil	1	8-ounce jar calamata olives, chopped
4	pita pockets		
1	package SeaPak® Garlic & Herb Shrimp	¼	cup fresh oregano, chopped
		1	teaspoon salt
1	pound feta cheese		

Brush both sides of each pita with olive oil, using half the oil. Set aside the remainder. Cook shrimp in the microwave according to package directions. In a bowl combine feta cheese, shrimp, olives, oregano and remaining olive oil. Mix and keep warm. In a preheated frying pan, toast each pita individually. Top with the shrimp mixture. Heat in a 350° oven for 5 minutes. Slice and serve.

Yield: 6-8 servings

Wollenberg's SeaPak® Garlic & Herb Shrimp Melt

2 pounds SeaPak® Garlic and Herb Shrimp

8 English muffins, sliced in half

8 ounces tomatoes (16 slices)

8 ounces provolone cheese (16 slices)

4 ounces roasted pepper purée

2 ounces mayonnaise
Salt and pepper to taste

Toast muffin halves lightly. Mix together roasted pepper and mayonnaise. Season to taste. Place tomato slice on each half muffin. Sauté shrimp and place 1½ ounces on top of tomato. Place a dollop of mayonnaise next. Top with a slice of cheese. Bake in oven until cheese is nicely melted. Serve.

Yield: 8 servings

Schmitz's Spanish Shrimp with Garlic

19½ ounces SeaPak® Garlic Herb Marinated Shrimp

½ cup olive oil

1 onion, diced

1 green pepper, diced

1 red pepper, diced

5 garlic cloves, chopped

1 teaspoon red pepper flakes to taste

2 tablespoons lemon juice
Salt and pepper to taste

1 teaspoon paprika

2 tablespoons parsley, minced

Heat oil in a large sauté pan over medium-high heat. Add the onions, peppers, garlic and pepper flakes and cook, stirring for about 2 minutes. Add the shrimp and cook for 2 minutes more until the shrimp are done. Squeeze in lemon juice and stir. Season to taste with salt and pepper. Divide shrimp into 6 ramekins or small casserole dishes. Sprinkle the paprika and parsley on top. May be served over rice or with bread.

Yield: 6 servings

Bales' Shrimp Fried Rice

2	tablespoons vegetable oil	2	tablespoons oyster sauce
½	cup yellow onion, diced	2	tablespoons soy sauce
1	tablespoon fresh gingerroot, grated	2	tablespoons oriental hot chili sauce or chili garlic sauce
6	cloves garlic, minced	2	tablespoons honey
½	cup white wine		

Rice

2	tablespoons vegetable oil	1	8-ounce can water chestnuts, sliced and drained
¾	cup yellow onions, diced		
12	ounces SeaPak® Garlic and Herb Shrimp	4	cups white rice, cooked and hot
		½	cup green onions, sliced
1	cup red peppers, diced	1	cup frozen peas, thawed
¾	cup carrots, julienned		

Combine oyster sauce, soy sauce, hot chili sauces and honey in a small bowl. Heat vegetable oil in a skillet until very hot. Add onions, garlic and ginger. Cook on high heat, stirring constantly, until the mixture is medium to dark brown in color (not black). Remove skillet from stove and carefully add white wine. Stir and return skillet to stove. Add remaining ingredients, making certain to scrape the bowl clean. Simmer for 5 minutes. Remove from heat and set aside. In a large skillet, heat vegetable oil and add onions. Cook until onions are golden brown and add shrimp. When shrimp is hot, add peppers, carrots and water chestnuts. Cook until soft. Add sauce, rice, green onions and peas. Cook for two minutes, stirring constantly.

Yield: 6 to 8 servings

Bales' Quesadillas
with Chile Sour Cream

Chile Sour Cream

8 ounces sour cream

1.5 ounces canned chipotle peppers or 1.5 ounces canned jalapeño peppers

1 ounce tomato sauce

Quesadillas

1 tablespoon butter

6 1-inch flour tortillas

12 ounces Monterey Jack cheese, shredded

3 ounces green onions, sliced

6 ounces red peppers, diced

12 ounces SeaPak® Marinated and Grilled Garlic Herb Shrimp (60-70 count)

2 ounces lettuce, shredded

3 ounces tomatoes, diced

1 ounce green onions, sliced

Combine all ingredients for the Chile Sour Cream and set aside. Melt the butter on a hot griddle or skillet. For each quesadilla, place one tortilla on the griddle and sprinkle with 2 ounces of cheese, ½ ounce of green onions and 1 ounce of red peppers. While the cheese is melting, place 2 ounces of shrimp on the griddle to brown. When the cheese has melted, and the shrimp has browned, place the shrimp on the tortilla in a line across the center. Fold the tortilla into thirds and cut diagonally across the center. Place the quesadilla on a plate with ⅓ of shredded lettuce, ½ ounce diced tomatoes, 1 #30 scoop of Chile Sour Cream and a pinch of sliced green onions.

Yield: 6 servings

O'Hara's Shrimp and Black Bean Fritter

2	cups flour	1	cup black beans, cooked and cooled
¾	cup cornstarch	1	pound SeaPak® Bourbon Shrimp
1	cup milk	3	tablespoons parsley, chopped
4	egg yolks	4	egg whites
4	teaspoons baking soda		
¼	teaspoon salt		

Sift the flour and cornstarch together. Slowly whisk in the milk. Stir in the yolks one at a time. Fold in the baking soda and salt. Add shrimp, black beans and parsley. Mix well. Let rest one hour. Just before service, gently fold in 4 stiffly beaten egg whites. Using a 1-ounce scoop, deep fat fry at 350° until golden brown and cooked through. Drain well.

Yield: 6 servings

Goellner's Rich's Ragin' Cajun Gumbo

½	pound chorizo sausage	1	(8-ounce) can red kidney beans, drained
1	package SeaPak® Garlic & Herb Shrimp (71-80 count)	1	(10-ounce) jar salsa (hot)
2	medium Spanish onions, sliced	2	teaspoons red pepper flakes
1	(8-ounce) can black beans, drained	1	(10-ounce) package instant rice
			Salt to taste
			Tabasco sauce to taste

Sauté chorizo in a nonstick pan for 2 minutes. Add onions and cook until translucent. Add shrimp and cook for an additional two minutes, stirring often. Mix in the beans and salsa. Bring to a light simmer and add red pepper flakes. Allow mixture to simmer while preparing the rice. Prepare rice according to package instructions. Remove from heat and fold into liquid mixture in saucepan. Add salt and Tabasco to taste.

Yield: 6 servings

Dietrich's Shrimp and Red Bliss Potato Salad

Salad

1	teaspoon salt
1½	pound red bliss potatoes
1½	pound mesquite shrimp
2	ounces oil

1	bunch scallions, whole, washed, thinly sliced
2	stalks celery, washed, diced
1	red bell pepper, seeded, diced

Dressing

½	cup silken tofu
3	tablespoons freshly squeezed lemon juice
2	tablespoons virgin olive oil

1	tablespoon Dijon mustard
3	tablespoons fresh tarragon, chopped
	Salt and pepper to taste

Put potatoes in a large pot with salted water and cook over high heat until the potatoes are just tender. Sauté shrimp in oil until translucent, drain and reserve. For the dressing, put all the ingredients into a food processor. Process until smooth and creamy, season to taste, reserve. When the potatoes are cool enough to handle, cut them into quarters. Transfer them to a large bowl, add the scallions and celery. Add the dressing and toss gently. Divide equally onto 6 serving plates and decorate with the diced pepper.

Yield: 6 servings

Duffy's Shrimp and Eggplant Napoleon Parmesan

2	large eggplant, peeled, sliced thin	2	pounds SeaPak® Lemon Pepper Shrimp
2	eggs	8	cups tomato sauce
1	cup milk	4	cups mozzarella cheese
2	cups flour	2	tablespoons Parmesan cheese
2	cups bread crumbs	2	tablespoons parsley, chopped

Beat the egg and milk together to create an egg wash. Dip the eggplant in the flour then egg wash and finish in bread crumbs. Deep-fry the eggplant and shrimp and lay on absorbent paper. Place one slice of eggplant on sizzle platter, top with shrimp and a little sauce. Place another slice of eggplant on top, add more shrimp and sauce. Top with one final slice of eggplant. Ladle tomato sauce on top, sprinkle with mozzarella cheese and bake in 350° oven for 10 minutes. Remove from oven and sprinkle with Parmesan and parsley.

Yield: 8 servings

Dietrich's Garlic and Herb Shrimp à la Grecque

2	ounces olive oil	1½	teaspoons fresh oregano
1½	pound SeaPak® Garlic and Herb Shrimp	3	tomatoes, diced
3	cloves garlic, chopped fine	18	calamata olives, pitted
		12	ounces feta cheese, crumbled

Sauté shrimp in oil. When barely translucent, add garlic and oregano. Add tomato and cook 2 minutes more. Add olives and heat through. Divide equally onto 6 plates and sprinkle with cheese. Serve immediately.

Yield: 6 servings

Jack Kane's Pink Vodka Sauce with Garlic & Herb Grilled/Marinated Shrimp over Spaghetti

Pink Vodka Sauce

2   ounces bacon, diced
1   ounce garlic, minced
2   ounces onion, diced
2   ounces vodka

18 ounces marinara sauce
6   ounces heavy cream
2   ounces Parmesan cheese

Shrimp/Spaghetti

3   ounces spaghetti
4   ounces SeaPak® Garlic and Herb Grilled and Marinated Shrimp

½   ounce Parmesan cheese
1   sprig fresh herbs

For Sauce: In a sauce pan sauté bacon until brown. Drain excess fat. Sauté onion and garlic with cooked bacon. Deglaze with vodka and reduce by half. Add marinara sauce and let simmer. Whisk in cream and Parmesan cheese. Season with salt and pepper.

For Assembly: Sauté 4 ounces SeaPak® Garlic and Herb Grilled and Marinated Shrimp. Add 4 ounces pink sauce over cooked shrimp. With a braising fork twirl 3 ounces of cooked spaghetti and place on the center of plate. Pour sauce with shrimp over pasta and garnish with fresh herbs and Parmesan cheese.

Yield: 6 servings

Ozga's
SeaPak® Shrimp Roll

1½ pounds short grain rice, washed	18 SeaPak® Jumbo Oven Crunchy Butterfly Shrimp
24 ounces water	
1 tablespoon sugar	½ head romaine lettuce, washed and dried
2 ounces rice wine vinegar	
6 seaweed sheets	1 avocado
	6 ounces soy sauce

Rice Preparation: Place rice and water in saucepan. Cover and cook over low heat for 20 minutes. Place in a bowl and allow to cool for about 15 minutes. In a small saucepan combine rice wine vinegar and sugar. Cook over low heat for 5 minutes. Season rice with the vinegar mixture and allow to rest for 15 minutes. Place shrimp on a baking sheet and place in a 435° oven for 10 to 12 minutes. Cut avocado in quarters lengthwise. Cut each piece in 5 wedges. Wrap rolling (sushi) mat with plastic wrap to keep rice from sticking.

Assembly of Roll: Lay the rolling mat on a cutting board. Then lay 1 sheet of seaweed in the middle of the mat (shinier side down). Wet your hand with cold water and take one handful of rice, placing it in the center of the seaweed sheet. Spread rice with your hands to cover the whole seaweed surface. Flip over so that the rice is face down to the rolling mat. Place 2 slices of avocado, 1 leaf of romaine and 3 shrimp lengthwise in the center of the sheet. Starting on the bottom side take the mat and begin rolling away from you, ensuring that the roll is tight. With a wet, sharp knife, cut the roll into 8 to 10 pieces. Place on a serving plate and serve with soy sauce for dipping.

Yield: 6 servings

Joni Bales' Louisiana-Style Shrimp Gumbo with Rice

2 tablespoons vegetable oil	2 teaspoons Worcestershire sauce
1 tablespoon garlic, minced	¾ cup tomatoes, diced
¾ cup yellow onion, diced	2 teaspoons Tabasco sauce
¾ cup carrots, diced	Dash cayenne pepper
¾ cup red pepper, diced	1 teaspoon black pepper
¾ cup celery, diced	1 teaspoon salt
2 teaspoons dried basil	10 ounces SeaPak® Garlic and Herb
2 teaspoons dried oregano	Shrimp (71-80 count)
2 teaspoons dried thyme	¾ cup fresh or frozen okra, sliced
½ cup butter	1 teaspoon filé powder
¾ cup flour	Prepared brown rice
5 cups chicken broth	

Heat oil in a skillet. Sauté onions and garlic until golden brown. Add celery, carrots, red pepper and dried herbs. Cook until tender. In a saucepan or a large skillet, melt butter. Add flour. Stirring constantly, cook until it is chocolate brown. Lower heat to medium. Using a whisk, incorporate the chicken stock 2 tablespoons at a time. Return pan to heat and simmer until it gets thick, stirring often. Add Worcestershire sauce, tomatoes, Tabasco sauce, cayenne, salt and pepper. Stir and add the vegetable mixture. When the mixture starts to boil again, add the shrimp and okra. Return to a boil and simmer for 5 minutes. Remove from heat and add filé powder.

Yield: 6 servings

Wollenberg's Shrimp Margarita Linguine with Buffalo Mozzarella

4 pounds linguine, cooked	1 ounce fresh basil
1½ pounds SeaPak® Garlic and Herb Shrimp	16 ounces plum tomatoes (slice into rings)
3 ounces olive oil	8 ounces marinara sauce
1 ounce garlic, chopped	Buffalo mozzarella

Sauté garlic in olive oil. Add shrimp and toss lightly. Add basil and tomatoes. Continue to sauté a few minutes and add marinara. Heat pasta in boiling water and drain well. Toss with shrimp mixture and add parsley. Serve in pasta bowls.

Yield: 8 servings

Wollenberg's Guiltless Shrimp Pasta Primavera

1½ pounds SeaPak® Garlic and Herb Shrimp	6 ounces artichoke hearts, quartered
4 pounds linguine, cooked	8 ounces canned whole tomatoes, roughly chopped
8 ounces carrots, julienned	4 ounces scallions, chopped
8 ounces red bell pepper, julienned	1 pint plain yogurt
8 ounces zucchini, julienned	4 ounces pesto

Sauté carrots, peppers and zucchini until they begin to cook slightly. Add artichokes and tomatoes and continue to cook. Add yogurt and pesto. Heat thoroughly. Toss all ingredients together including scallions. Serve immediately.

Serving Suggestion: Serve with garlic toast and Parmesan cheese.

Yield: 8 servings

Duffy's Rigatoni with Garlic and Herb Shrimp Ragu

4	tablespoons olive oil
2	pounds SeaPak® Garlic and Herb Shrimp
1	cup red onion, diced
1	cup carrots, diced
1	cup celery, diced
1	cup mushroom, diced

4	cups canned tomatoes, chopped
1	cup white wine
24	ounces rigatoni pasta, cooked
½	cup Parmesan cheese
2	tablespoons parsley, chopped
	Salt and pepper to taste

Heat half of the oil in a skillet and sauté shrimp for 2 minutes. Remove from skillet and hold. Add the rest of the oil and sauté the carrot, onion, celery and mushroom. Add tomatoes and wine to the skillet and reduce by half. Toss the shrimp and pasta into the sauce and heat. Add cheese and parsley. Season to taste.

Yield: 8 servings

NOTES

Index

C

Cabbage

Casseroles

Cheese

Clams

Cobia

Condiments & Sauces

Corn

Crab